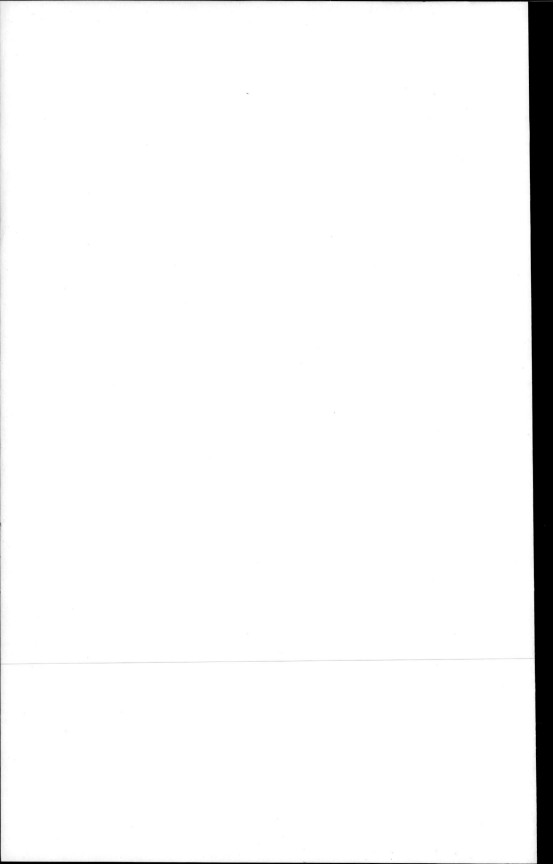

APPLIED AUDIOLOGY FOR CHILDREN

Second Edition

APPLIED AUDIOLOGY

FOR

CHILDREN

By

D. M. C. DALE

Dip.Ed. (N.Z.), Ph.D. (Manchester)

*Senior Lecturer in the Education
of Deaf and Partially Hearing Children
Department of Child Development
London University Institute of Education
London, England*

With a Foreword by

Professor Sir Alexander Ewing

*The University of Manchester
Manchester, England*

CHARLES C THOMAS · PUBLISHER
Springfield · Illinois · U.S.A.

Published and Distributed Throughout the World by

CHARLES C THOMAS • PUBLISHER

BANNERSTONE HOUSE

301-327 East Lawrence Avenue, Springfield, Illinois, U.S.A.

NATCHEZ PLANTATION HOUSE

735 North Atlantic Boulevard, Fort Lauderdale, Florida, U.S.A.

First Edition, 1962

Second Edition, 1967

With THOMAS BOOKS *careful attention is given to all details of manufacturing and design. It is the Publisher's desire to present books that are satisfactory as to their physical qualities and artistic possibilities and appropriate for their particular use.* THOMAS BOOKS *will be true to those laws of quality that assure a good name and good will.*

Printed in the United States of America
P-4

FOREWORD

It gives me great pleasure to have an opportunity to recommend this book. As its title indicates it has been written as a source of immediate and practical help both to professional workers who have responsibility for all categories of hearing-impaired children and to parents. Its very great merit is the skill with which Dr. Dale has summarised and explained (for the most part in everyday language) results of modern research on hearing, speech and deafness by many workers, spot-lighting their relevance to the day-to-day needs and problems of children with varying degrees and types of deafness.

Treating in the same way the results of his own extensive experience as investigator and teacher, in New Zealand and in England, he has described tests of capacity to hear speech and to benefit from amplification for children of different ages, ways of ensuring that hearing aids are maintained in good order, methods of auditory training and the information that is needed by teachers in ordinary schools who have pupils with defective hearing.

Dr. Dale shows keen awareness of an urgent need to give deaf children as full experience of hearing as contemporary electronics make physically possible; widening its scope to make all possible sounds of daily life meaningful, even although many of the children can be enabled to hear them a good deal less completely than ordinary people. Some of his case histories are particularly valuable and relevant to this point. His own research, both in England and New Zealand, has taught him that parents and teachers and children themselves, need special training, knowledge and skill if the hearing aids are to be used to full advantage and throughout children's waking hours.

The book includes numerous illustrations. A notable example is a series of photographs of visible speech recordings that show scientifically (in terms of spectrographic analysis) just how people can help hearing aid users by the manner of their phonation and articulation. There is an excellent index and bibliography.

I have come to believe in recent years that from the standpoint of education audiology is as yet too much based on work with deafened adults. Dr. Dale's book is one of the first to deal specifically with the audiological problems of children—at home and at school—who do not hear normally while they are growing up.

The University,   A. W. G. Ewing
Manchester, England

PREFACE TO THE SECOND EDITION

In this Second Edition, a few changes have been made. Information on speech tests and hearing aids has been brought up to date and some inaccuracies in the earlier text have been corrected. The International Audiometric Zero was standardised in 1964 and reference to it is now included in this book.

Perhaps the most significant recent development in applying basic audiological principles to the education of children with defective hearing has been the evolving of the *listening-reading-speaking method*. Both the individual and the group technique are now described in some detail in Chapter 8.

Since writing this book, my conviction that wherever possible, deaf and partially hearing children should mix freely and regularly with normally hearing children both in and out of school has been more and more strengthened. The primary purposes, of course, are social and educational, but audiologically too it stands to reason that to be surrounded for most of the day by children who are using normal patterns of speech can only be of advantage to the hearing impaired child.

D. M. C. DALE
London University
Institute of Education

PREFACE TO THE FIRST EDITION

THIS BOOK is written to help teachers, parents, doctors, and workers in audiology clinics make the most use of sound in the educational and social treatment of deafness.

There are numerous factors which seem to assist deaf children to overcome their communication difficulties. These might include: the tremendous contribution which well trained parents can make during the child's early years; the importance of well equipped schools, and able headmasters who are genuinely interested in deaf children; well trained teachers; the closest possible liaison between home and school; and regular association with normally hearing children who have been shown how best to help the deaf ones. The use of hearing aids should be viewed in relation to these other factors. For many children and adults an aid can enable them to carry on a virtually normal conversational life which would be quite impossible without it. For others, where the deafness is more severe, the effect of wearing a hearing aid is neither so noticeable nor so immediate. Further evidence is given in this book, however, of the benefit which hearing aids can be, even to children and adults who are profoundly deaf.

It is felt that if those who work in this field possess an elementary knowledge of the nature of sound, and of the means of amplifying it and presenting it to deaf children, they will be better able to ensure that the children receive the most intelligible, the most meaningful, and the most continuous experience of sound, that their residual capacity to hear permits.

Very grateful acknowledgment is made to the Medical Research Council for financial assistance given while conducting much of the research reported in this book. I wish to thank also Professor Sir Alexander Ewing, and members of the staff of the Department of Audiology and Education of the Deaf, at The University of Manchester, for their assistance at all times. Numerous principals of schools for the deaf in England, Holland,

Australia, and New Zealand, together with their teachers and deaf children, have been very kind and helpful to me, and I am greatly indebted to them all for this. The late Dr. C. V. Hudgins, Clarke School for the Deaf, Massachusetts, very kindly gave assistance with interpreting the sonagrams. Father A. van Uden, Instituut voor Doven, St. Michiels Gestel, Holland, is responsible for most of the information in the section on music for deaf children. Finally, Dr. B. B. Harold, Assistant Director, Commonwealth Acoustic Laboratories, Sydney, has given very freely of his time and information, and has made valued criticisms of several sections of the text.

D. M. C. DALE
Teachers' College
Christchurch, N.Z.

CONTENTS

ILLUSTRATIONS

APPLIED AUDIOLOGY FOR CHILDREN

Chapter 1

SOUND AMPLIFICATION

THE NATURE OF SOUND

Sound is produced when there are rapid changes in air pressure. It thus originates in matter that is *vibrating*. Common vibrating objects are strings, reeds and membranes. When a tuning fork is struck, the prongs vibrate until they finally come to rest again. If the movement of one prong is examined it may be seen that it travels backwards and forwards as in Figure 1. As the prong moves out, it pushes the air molecules in front of it into a little group. This is known as a *compression*. When the prong moves back and past its original position it creates a kind of vacuum behind it and this is called a *rarefaction*. As the prong moves outwards again, another compression results, and as long as it vibrates, compressions and rarefactions occur in the air.

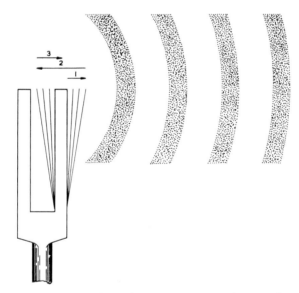

Figure 1. Compressions and rarefactions emanating from a vibrating source.

When the pulsations of air reach the ear, they are perceived as sound. If they come very rapidly, the sound heard is a high pitched one. If the pulsations come less frequently the sound is said to be low in *pitch*. Each time the prong of the fork (or the string of the violin, etc.) vibrates back and forth, and back again to its original position (Fig. 1. Movements 1, 2 and 3), it is said to have completed one *cycle*. A more accurate method of describing sounds than simply saying they are high or low pitched, is to measure the number of cycles occurring in the vibrating object every second, and to express the number in terms of *frequency* (frequency being the number of cycles per second). Pitch is a subjective quality and does not imply numerical value, whereas frequency is an objective physical measure. When middle C on the piano is played, for example, the appropriate string moves back and right forward and then back again to its original position 256 times in every second. Middle C is therefore said to be a sound of 256 cycles per second (c.p.s.). The human ear is capable of perceiving sounds from as low as 20 c.p.s. to as high as 20,000 c.p.s. As will be emphasised later, however, the limited range in which the important components of speech sounds occur, lies between 300 and 3,000 c.p.s.

ELECTRICAL AMPLIFICATION OF SOUND

The principle involved in making sounds louder is the same in nearly all electrical amplifying systems whether they be public address systems at fair grounds, in theatres or railway stations, or the type employed in most varieties of hearing aids. Such amplifying systems usually contain three parts: (a) a *microphone*; (b) an *amplifier*, and (c) a *receiver* or *speaker* (Fig. 2).

Sound travels through the air. As the sound wave impinges on the microphone, the pressure variations are transformed into voltage signals which are passed through the amplifier. The am-

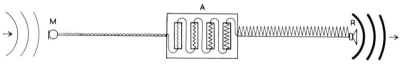
Figure 2. The principle of electrical amplification of sound.

plifier contains *valves* or in the modern individual hearing aid, *transistors*. The function of the valves or transistors is to make electrical waves larger, i.e., they amplify the wave. The function of the receiver is to convert this enlarged electrical wave back into sound pressure—it is like a microphone working in reverse. Because the wave is much larger than the original, the sound produced by the receiver is louder than the sound which impinged upon the microphone. This, of course, is what the crowd or the audience or the deaf patient requires.

It is relatively easy to identify these three components in any hearing aids being used (Fig. 3).

INPUT, GAIN AND OUTPUT

Input

The optimum input to a hearing aid microphone is about 70 db. above .0002 dynes per cm ^{2}. That is, about the level of conversational speech at a distance of three feet. A common fault of teachers and parents is that they speak much too loudly into the hearing aid. With 70 db. (or greater) input, and full volume control, the output stage is likely to *overload*. Such overloading causes distortion of the speech and frequently a *reduction* in intelligibility rather than the desired increase.

In poor acoustic conditions, it is wise to keep the voice at a reasonably high level, however, to achieve a good *signal to noise* ratio: i.e., plenty of voice entering the microphone excludes or at least *masks out* the quieter background noises.

It is possible, by practising with a sound level meter, to maintain the desired level of input to the microphone. In concentrating on keeping the correct level, however, one must be careful not to allow one's voice to become flat and uninteresting. Radio and television announcers usually have excellently controlled and modulated voices.

One should not be too concerned if "occasionally" the voice is raised above the best level. If, for example, a story is being told in which one of the characters is required to shout, then by all means let him shout. The word or words shouted may be distorted, but the story will not be spoilt by an unnatural presenta-

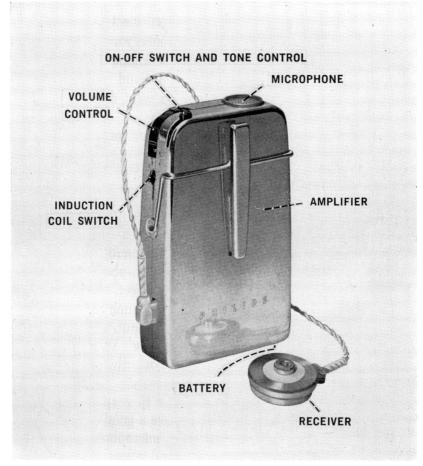

Figure 3. Microphone, amplifier and receiver of one common type of hearing aid.

tion. One would have to consider abandoning the use of hearing aids if they unduly inhibited the teacher's style in the presentation of lessons.

Using the correct input level most of the time is just one of many ways of ensuring that the children hear the clearest possible pattern of speech.

Gain

Hearing aids do not make all sounds equally loud, e.g., there is usually more emphasis given to the sounds between 750 and 3,000 c.p.s. than to the frequencies above or below this range (Fig. 4). Many hearing aids *peak* [have their maximum amplification] at 1,000 or 1,500 c.p.s. Because of this, and because 1,000 c.p.s. is regarded as near the middle of the speech frequency range, the *gain* of a hearing aid is usually referred to as the amplification it gives at 1,000 c.p.s. when switched to maximum. The input must be such that the output is not distorted.

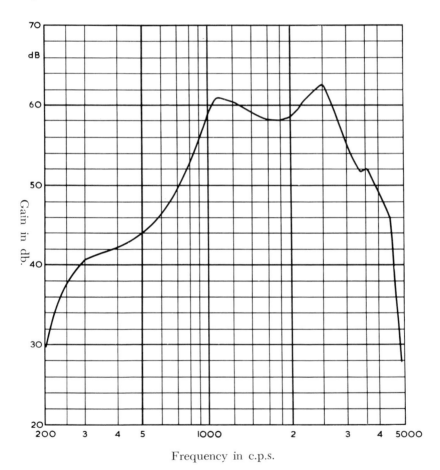

Figure 4. Response curve of a hearing aid.

Output

The level of sound which comes from a hearing aid receiver is known as the *output* of the hearing aid. It may be calculated by the simple formula:

$$\text{Input} + \text{Gain} = \text{Output}.$$

Thus if 60 db. of sound is put into the microphone, and the aid amplifies this by 45 db., then the output of the aid is 105 db. (60 db. + 45 db. = 105 db.).

The majority of the better makes of individual hearing aids have a maximum output of 125 db. above .0002 dynes/cm². This output is quite adequate for the majority of hearing aid users but for the profoundly and subtotally deaf children, it is often necessary to give greater output. This is frequently though not necessarily done by increasing the battery tension. Makers of hearing aids usually state that if a 1.5 volt battery gives a maximum output of 125 db., 3 volts will give a maximum output of 130 db. and 4 volts a maximum output of 135 db. above .0002 dynes/cm².

Simply increasing the amplification, however, is not always what is required. Often, for profoundly deaf children, it seems most desirable to give the lower frequencies of the hearing aids more response, i.e., in the region where a remnant of hearing remains, rather than just to increase the overall output.[166, 128]

It will be shown later that a knowledge of the output of hearing aids is very important to all teachers of the deaf, and is particularly so for those teachers who deal with young deaf children.

RESPONSE CURVES

It is possible to measure the amount of amplification given by a hearing aid at different frequencies and to plot these measurements on a graph. Such data (Fig. 4) are known as the *response curve* or the *frequency characteristics* of a hearing aid.

The invention of the audiometer made it possible to measure with accuracy, a person's threshold of audibility for pure tones throughout a wide range of frequencies. Quite soon after this, the plausible hypothesis was advanced that if one could compensate in amplification the patient's hearing loss at each frequency, then near normal hearing should result. This practice was known as *selective amplification* or *audiogram fitting*, and seems to have received favourable consideration from nearly all audiologists during the 1930's and early 1940's. Towards the end of World War II, however, a large-scale research was initiated in the Electro-Acoustic Laboratories at Harvard University into the requirements of hearing aids. Evidence was produced regarding optimum frequency characteristics of hearing aids. ". . . quite at variance with current thought and practice at the Aural Rehabilitation Hospitals, and with the preconceived ideas of the writers themselves." [30] The principles of selective amplification were shown not to represent the best response curves for hearing aids. A uniform frequency characteristic that could be varied by a tone control between a flat and a moderate accentuation of the high tones, proved to be the most satisfactory response for all or nearly all cases of hearing loss. Thus for the usual hard of hearing patient any detailed "fitting" of hearing aids was, the report said, "wasteful of time and effort." For the unusual and difficult cases, more elaborate selective tests were considered appropriate. Carhart [15] described a battery of these tests which he used in the selection of: (a) the best hearing aid from several instruments, and (b) the aid most suitable for the patient. These involved a consideration of certain dimensions of hearing aid performance—sensitivity or gain, signal to noise ratio, and efficiency in discriminating small sound differences. It was presupposed that patients possessed an adequate language background before such tests were attempted.

The Committee on Electro-Acoustics of the Medical Research Council of Great Britain published the results of an investigation similar to the Harvard study in 1947.[137] Experiments designed to determine the characteristics of a hearing aid suitable for general use were carried out during 1945 with sixty-three adult patients at the Department of Education of the Deaf at Manchester University and 165 patients in the Otological Research Unit at the National Hospital, London. The results indicated: (a) that a cut off above 4,000 c.p.s. was not detrimental to intelligibility, and (b), like the Harvard Report, that in order to achieve the best results the amplification between 750 and 4,000 c.p.s. should be uniform or should increase with frequency.

Groen and Tappin [81] observed the reactions of approximately one hundred patients after they had listened with each of five hearing aids possessing different response characteristics. The results obtained, however, differed little from those of the Harvard and Medical Research Council studies. Patients preferred the hearing aid which gave some reduction to the low tones and a flat characteristic to the higher tones with a cut off at approximately 4,000 cycles. They found that when using an aid which amplified the lower tones (from 125-500 c.p.s.) as well as the higher ones, patients complained of considerable distortion. As suggested earlier, however, profoundly deaf patients do require low frequency amplification if they are to hear at all. A very interesting recent development has been in the field of *signal processing*. Instruments have been produced which can transpose the higher frequency sounds—which are necessary for hearing speech intelligibly—to the lower frequency area.[110, 161, 167] Pimonow, for example, used ten band pass channels throughout the essential speech frequency area, and drove ten low frequency generators with the output of each. Johansson has also reported favourably on results obtained with his transposer and a more thorough evaluation of the instrument is now in progress in several countries.[111]

LIMITING THE OUTPUT OF HEARING AIDS

The earliest hearing aids tended to boost both loud and soft sounds by the same amount. If, for example, a sound of 30 db. was presented to these aids, it might be amplified by 50 db. (to 80 db.). A sound of 70 db. would also be amplified by the same amount, so that the output would then be 120 db. Apart from the fact that such loud sounds could be most unpleasant for the wearer, there was also a detrimental effect on intelligibility. It was realised that a better form of *limiting* should be incorporated in hearing aids.

Licklider [5] showed that if a communication system had "insufficient amplitude handling capacity to pass the peaks of speech, but at the same time provided an adequate intensity level, maximum intelligibility could be obtained by clipping off the peaks

and using the available power for the remainder of the wave."
He applied this principle to radio transmitters and to hearing
aids and found, for example, that although 24 db. of peak
clipping did affect the quality of the speech reproduced,
there was no detrimental effect on speech intelligibility. In hearing aids, of course, the amplitude handling capability of the
system is limited by the listener's threshold of discomfort. By
introducing peak clipping it was now possible for hearing aid
users to perceive the quieter sounds of speech undistorted and at
louder levels than ever before and therefore attain greater intelligibility than was possible in aids containing undistorted amplifying systems.

Two years later, Hudgins and others [98] reported the results of
a further investigation at Harvard. The comparative performance
of four hearing aids was studied. Two were commercial aids without limiting, one was an experimental wearable hearing aid designed in the Electro-Acoustic Laboratory and including a *compression* type of automatic volume control and the fourth was a
Master Hearing Aid with variable characteristics. The experimental aid proved superior to the commercial aids particularly
when the input signal was in excess of 70 db. This research re-
emphasized both the feasibility and desirability of using some
form of limitation in individual hearing aids such as peak clipping
or a compression type of AVC.

With compression amplification, the wave is *gradually* reduced
at the top (i.e., the loudest sounds), as distinct from the sharp
cut off used in peak clipping (Fig. 5). The effect of such gradual
limitation is alleged to give a more natural sound to the amplified
speech than does peak clipping. As far as intelligibility is concerned, however, there does not appear to be a great deal of difference between the two types of limiting. To date, no experiment seems to have been conducted to show conclusively whether
one method is superior to the other.

An interesting little research in this field of optimum hearing
aid characteristics was made by Edgardh.[41] He effected a dynamic equalisation of the vowels and consonants by what he
called "extreme limitation." The limitation employed by Edgardh
appeared to differ in two respects from the normal compression

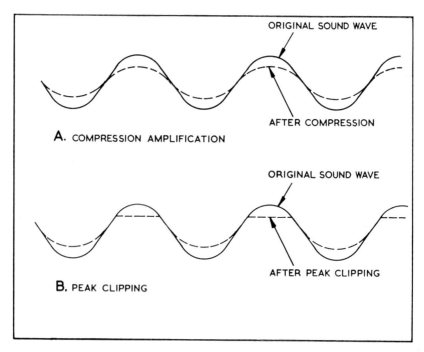

ORIGINAL SOUND WAVE

AFTER COMPRESSION

A. COMPRESSION AMPLIFICATION

ORIGINAL SOUND WAVE

AFTER PEAK CLIPPING

B. PEAK CLIPPING

Figure 5. Sound limitation in hearing aids.

type of amplification. Instead of compressing say, the top 10 db. of the maximum peaks of the input signals into approximately 1 db., Edgardh's extreme limitation frequently compressed the maximum 30 db. into about 3. Secondly, in order to obtain maximum amplification for the consonants, the *release time* was reduced from between 100 and 400 milliseconds, to approximately 20 milliseconds. One noticeable effect when this limitation was used was that each breath taken by the speaker was amplified to a loud gasp, and this Edgardh said, was "far from pleasing aesthetically." Despite the distortion of the speech, however, he found no adverse effect on the intelligibility of either male or female voices.

Reference Levels

Physicists, when they design sound producing apparatus, use as their reference level an extremely slight sound pressure which is equivalent to .0002 dynes/cm^2. This point was first selected because it was the quietest level of a 1,000 c.p.s. tone which could be heard in the free field by highly trained listeners.

To be audible to untrained listeners with average hearing, who are using earphones, it has been found that sounds need to be boosted by about 10 db. above .0002 dynes/cm ^{2} * at 1000 c.p.s. At 250 c.p.s. the tone must be increased by about 28 db. before it can be heard, whilst a really low-pitched sound, like 125 c.p.s. requires nearly 50 db. above .0002 dynes/cm^2 to make it audible (Fig. 6). The differences do, of course, vary with different earphones. In making an instrument to test human hearing at various frequencies, (the audiometer) manufacturers cannot therefore use a scale which begins at .0002 dynes/cm^2 They take the points where each tone, through earphones, becomes audible to the average human ear, and call it *clinical zero*, i.e., the beginning of their decibel scale. The clinical zeros have now been standardised through the International Standards Organisation.[29] The ISO levels are similar to those which were previously used as the British Standard,[11] and are approximately 10 db. more severe than those recommended by the American Medical Association in 1951. This fact should be borne in mind when comparing hearing losses quoted in this book, i.e., a hearing loss of 80 db. using an audiometer calibrated on the AMA scale is equivalent to a 90 db. hearing loss as measured by a British (or European) instrument.

The ISO line on the graph in Fig. 6 is the *threshold of audibility*. It is this line which appears as the straight "0" line along the top of present day audiograms. Two zeros are thus being used in audiology, one is that of .0002 dynes per cm^2 and the other is the normal threshold of detectability. The former applies primarily to the outputs of hearing aids, the latter to audiometers,† and to audiograms. When relating outputs to audiogram data (as for example when setting the output of a speech training hearing aid), it is necessary to deduct 15 db. from the marked output. This correction ensures that one is then calculating on

---

* A dyne is a unit of force. One gram under the pull of gravity exerts a force of 980 dynes, at sea level and certain latitudes. (From Wever, E. G. (1957): *Theory of Hearing*. New York, John Wiley and Sons, Inc., p. 444.)

† Both speech and pure tone circuits.

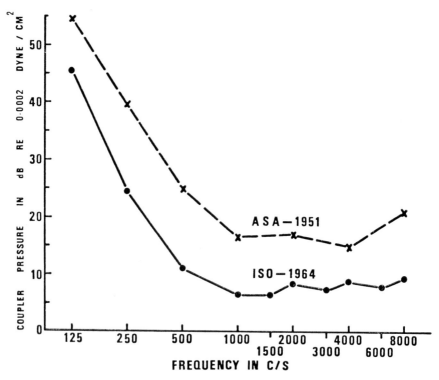

Figure 6. Discrepancies between .0002 dynes per cm² and International Audiometric Zero.

approximately the same scale, since 15 db. is roughly the average difference between the two levels throughout the speech range.

HEARING AIDS OF DIFFERENT TYPES

It is proposed here to discuss four types of hearing aids in common use at the present time: the individual wearable hearing aid, group hearing aids, hearing aids incorporating an induction coil, and speech training aids.

Individual Wearable Hearing Aids

The ultimate development of this type of hearing aid will be one which fits completely inside the ear and for those people who benefit from *binaural listening*, one will be worn in each ear.[78] One or two manufacturers have produced aids of this type already, but they have not so far proved very successful. Three difficulties with them are: (a) to produce them small enough to fit comfortably within the ear; (b) to obtain an effective seal around the mould which will prevent *acoustic feedback* (leakage of sound from the receiver to the microphone)—the receiver and microphone are of necessity placed within less than an inch of one another in such small instruments, and (c) when using such miniature components, to provide the most desirable frequency response at the receiver. It is felt to be only a matter of time, however, before such difficulties are overcome.

Much more success has been achieved with the slightly larger hearing aids worn behind the ear (Fig. 7-A) or concealed in spectacles (Fig. 7-B), brooches, ear-rings, hairclips, etc. These aids can, however, be expensive to buy and to maintain and service, and with little children, can be easily lost.

The most common type of individual hearing aid is that which has the microphone, amplifier, and battery (or batteries) all in one compartment which is worn usually on the chest, and a cord which leads to the receiver and individual ear insert or mould (Fig. 7-C). There are numerous makes and varieties of these. The better ones perform extremely well, are durable, aesthetic and are light enough that they can be worn without the wearers noticing that they are there. There is no virtue in reducing the size of this type of hearing aid further since such tiny aids would be too easily lost.

The question of the advantages of binaural listening, has not yet been satisfactorily resolved.[32] A number of writers have observed a lowering of the threshold of detectability of approximately 3 db. when either speech or pure tones are listened to first with one ear and then with both. In many cases, the ability to locate the source of sound improves when listening binaurally. There is also a growing body of evidence that many children and adults prefer to use two aids rather than just one. Neurologists state that the use of binaural aids seems reasonable to them. When word list tests of hearing are used, however, the differences in scores obtained when using monaural and binaural aids, are seldom significantly different statistically.[9b, c]

One hearing aid can be connected to two receivers by a 'Y'

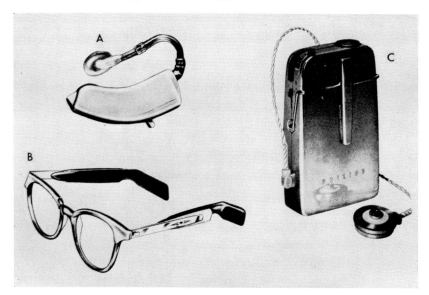

Figure 7. Individual hearing aids of various types.

cord. Although this is not true binaural listening, a number of children whose hearing losses are not too severe and almost identical in both ears, have reported favourably on it, and it is of course less costly than providing two hearing aids.

Group Hearing Aids

Group hearing aids seem first to have been designed in the late 1920's and early 1930's. Today, there are a variety of types of such aids. All are expensive.

The advantages of group hearing aids are that, if properly used, they enable the children to hear loud sound in both ears with better high and low frequency response. The disadvantages are the restriction of movement which they place on both child and teacher. N. E. Murray [147] has stated:

"Almost all attempts to improve the flexibility and use of group hearing aids are partial steps towards an individual aid. If the individual aid can reach technical efficiency comparable with group aids, then the individual aid is obviously the instrument of choice for educational work."

If a collar or head microphone is used the teacher is enabled to speak close to it. Distance from the microphone does, of course, affect speech intelligibility, and where classrooms are noisy and reverberant, can be the deciding factor in whether aids are of benefit or are not.

The fact that the children must be sitting down when using group aids renders them of limited value for young children. From about six years of age onwards, however, group hearing aids are more practical and their use in schools and classes for the deaf and partially hearing is fairly common. Suggestions for using group hearing aids are included in Chapter 8.

The Induction Loop System

Most of the better makes of individual hearing aid today incorporate an induction coil for use with this system. Very roughly, induced sound for hearing aid wearers is used in the following manner. A microphone is coupled to an amplifier and from the amplifier a *loop* of wire runs around the room (Fig. 8). When the power is switched on, the current flow in the wire creates a magnetic field within the loop (and for some distance outside it). When a person speaks into the microphone, the sound wave is turned into a voltage signal and passes to the amplifier where it is boosted. This enlarged signal then runs into the loop of wire and is *transmitted* within the magnetic field, i.e., the electrical impulse has now become a radio wave. This radio wave is picked up or, more correctly, "induced into" the hearing aid by the induction coil (a tiny coil of copper wire). It is thus changed back to a voltage signal, and this eventually passes up to the receiver of the aid and is reconverted to a sound wave again.

By using the induction system, the speaker is within a few inches of the microphone and the distance between him and the child is spanned with radio waves. Acoustic conditions are thus by-passed and the speech which is heard by this method in quite noisy and reverberant classrooms is clear and undistorted.

Although the child heard the teacher with beautiful clarity, it had not been possible for him to hear his own voice at all. This is such a serious limitation that the use of such a system in the normal classroom situation cannot be recommended. Hearing aids have been produced which are capable of being switched: (a) to

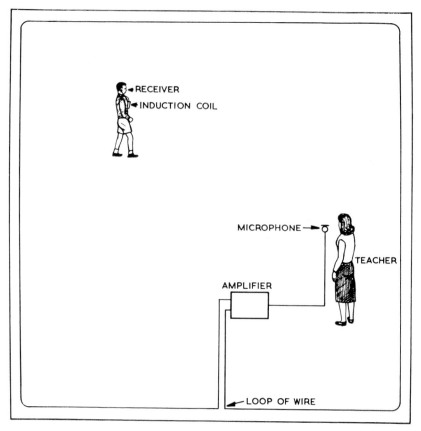

Figure 8. The induction system.

the induction coil; (b) to the microphone of the aid, and (c) to a position where both the induction coil and the hearing aid were in action at the same time. When using this third position, the child is supposed to hear the teacher's voice on the induction coil and his own voice via the microphone of his own aid. By switching in the sensitive little microphones of the individual hearing aids, however, one simultaneously switches in all the background noise and acoustic disturbance which the "loop system" so successfully eliminates. In a normal, noisy little infant room, for example, it is not possible to determine any difference between the positions—microphone plus "loop," and microphone only. To put it another way, interference picked up by the microphone masks out the clear speech which comes through the induction system.

Some contend that very good acoustic treatment of the rooms should eliminate the ambient noise which is being amplified. Eventually, some form of "walkie-talkie" apparatus may be developed which will enable two-way communication by radio waves.

In ordinary school classrooms, at school assemblies, in ballet, eurhythmical work, etc., i.e., where mostly only one-way communication is required, induction loop systems have proved extremely effective. Teachers should ensure that the younger children have their aids switched on to the "loop" position at the beginning of each session, and switched back to normal listening at the conclusion. Small *transmitter microphones* have been produced for use with loudspeakers in theatres and with other public address systems. They seem to have distinct possibilities for hearing aid users in the school situations mentioned above. Teachers can wear the transmitter microphones and be free of the lead which normally connects them to the amplifier and induction loop. One objection to them at the moment is economic—both the purchase price and the running costs are at present too high.

Loop systems can also be very useful when attached to television sets (and to radios provided the child is not too deaf). When using induction loops in this way, it is not necessary to purchase a microphone or amplifier. If it is desired to use the induction coil for *speech* in the home, then a microphone and an amplifier are necessary. It must be said, however, that the use of the system in this way has not proved very successful. One does not obtain clear speech by induction, unless one speaks close to the microphone. This means, therefore, that the microphone must be passed from one speaker to another, and at meal times or when sitting in the lounge at night, etc., this does not prove practical. If, as is normally done, the microphone is placed in the middle of the table or the middle of the room, then speakers are mostly so far away from it that the deaf person is not any better off than when wearing his ordinary hearing aid. Many parents who bought microphones and amplifiers in good faith are now trying to sell them again.

Speech Training Hearing Aids

Description. Speech training aids are table model, mains or battery operated individual aids (Fig. 9). One which is common in Commonwealth schools for the deaf is an aid which was manufactured by a commercial firm to specifications suggested by the Department of Education of the Deaf at the University of Manchester.[112] Such hearing aids have a frequency response which is more or less flat from 750 to 8,000 c.p.s. with a monitoring switch for each ear marked in 5 db. steps up to a maximum output of 135 dbs. above .0002 dynes/cm^2. They also possess an input level meter, a gain control, and it is possible to connect a radiogram or radio to them.

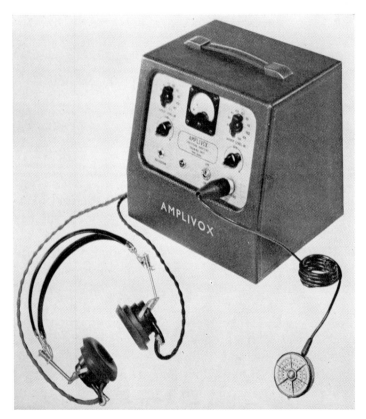

Figure 9. A speech training hearing aid.

Many of the methods which we use in teaching speech are by no means new, and provide at best only an approximation of the true patterns or elements required. An instrument which may one day be designed for speech teaching, is one which would be capable of analysing short samples of speech as accurately as is done by the Sonagraph (Fig. 21), but which is capable of making such analysis instantaneously and of retaining the display for several seconds, if necessary. By giving a child the correct pattern (either on another screen or on a chart), it would be possible for him to practise until he had produced the same shape on his screen, i.e., he would monitor with his eye in the same way as the normally hearing child monitors with his ear.

The possibilities of such an instrument as that suggested above, are quite exciting. One can imagine for example, that profoundly deaf infants could become interested in the visual patterns which they could make on the screen with their voices, and could experiment much more purposefully. Children and adults too should find this a real aid to assist in obtaining intelligible speech.

Class teachers who do not have the assistance of aides or helpers find difficulty in making use of speech training aids. "How can we take one child for individual work and at the same time, keep the rest of the class *usefully* employed?" they ask. It is possible to do one session of individual work each week, but to try to get an hour or so every day is extremely difficult. As a result of this, many of the speech training aids bought by schools are not used at all regularly.

If it is agreed that individual speech and auditory training work is valuable, there seem two possible means of providing it. One is by using a speech and auditory training specialist within the school who takes children from their classrooms for individual work. This method has the advantage that an experienced teacher is able to achieve much more in a given time than is an inexperienced one. There are some drawbacks, however. No matter how close the liaison between class teacher and specialist, the class teacher never really seems to obtain the exact information about each child's speech and hearing abilities and disabilities, which will be of most use to her when she is taking the class for the daily group speech lesson and at other times during the day. "Teaching the deaf to speak" is one of the most fascinating aspects of our work and one which many teachers, quite understandably, are loathe to relinquish to someone else.

A second method, which involves one teacher being used in a peripatetic capacity, seems to have possibilities. One teacher, essentially an able, experienced and energetic one, goes to, say, four classes for one hour each day and takes subjects decided upon by herself and the class teacher. Whilst she does this, the class teacher takes two (or three) children at a time to a quiet room nearby and does individual speech improvement and auditory training work. On one occasion it was possible to run a similar scheme on an experimental basis, for a four week period.

When asked to comment on the scheme at the end of the four-week period, the three class teachers wrote:

> 1. ". . . . Even in the short and experimental period the scheme was in operation, the children's speech improved noticeably and for the first time a really satisfactory and accurate assessment of speech and hearing could be made."
>
> 2. "Once we'd got organised it was wonderful. Quite a few of the parents commented on the speech improvement. . . . The children themselves enjoyed the individual work. Afterwards they would ask why we were not still doing it. . . ."
>
> 3. ". . . . I'm quite certain that peripatetic teachers can be of value and I'm looking forward to the time when we have another on our staff."

Such use of speech or voice training hearing aids may require additional staffing. If existing classes are not too large, however, it seems likely that by increasing the size of the classes a little, no increase in establishment should be necessary.

Chapter 2

THE MEASUREMENT OF HEARING

THIS CHAPTER deals with the importance of testing; a description of pure tone and speech tests of hearing; and a discussion of the various steps involved in a clinical test of a child's hearing. No mention is made here of three very interesting methods of testing which have been well described elsewhere, namely, psycho-galvanic skin response (PGSR) tests,[84, 13, 2, 22, 82, 85, 104, 125, 169, 178] the use of electroencephalography (EEG),[35, 36, 124, 138, 177, 202, 205] and screening tests for pre-school [59] and school aged children.[139]

Educationalists and psychologists are realising more and more the importance of keeping careful records of all aspects of children's capacities.

"To teach arithmetic to Richard or geography to George, it is not sufficient to know just the principles of arithmetic or the facts of geography. The teacher must also know Richard and George." [75]

In addition to the documentation of educational, psychological, medical and social data, if one intends to obtain a full picture of a "deaf" child, it is very necessary to have an accurate assessment of his hearing for speech and for pure tones. It is not sufficient now to know just that a child is "deaf" or is "partially hearing." A teacher of a very deaf class should be able to think of each member of the group and say, for example, "Meg has a 100 db. loss, yet she can do an amazing amount with the hearing she has retained, e.g., she can discriminate between six pairs of vowels, loves organ music, can detect quite slight changes in pitch and in rhythm, can identify me from the rest of my class by the quality of my voice, and always lets me know as soon as her hearing aid is not working. John, on the other hand, has a 95 db. loss, yet doesn't seem to have much discrimination at all—he has poor hearing for vowels, he can sometimes differentiate between sounds of widely dissimilar pitch, but as often as not gets quite confused. He doesn't like wearing his aid—quite understandably I suppose, etc." When possessing such information for all the class, this teacher would never ask any child to do the impossible when directing his listening, nor would she waste time giving experiences of listening which were so easy for a child that they bored him. In addition, of course, this knowledge assists the teacher when she reviews individual progress. Although all the class may have very similar pure tone losses the amount of help that their hearing is likely to have been to them must be considered in relation to the other factors of age, intelligence, home background, etc.

In addition to the tests such as those described later, teachers should continually be asking themselves "I wonder if Billy can hear this, or Peter hear that?" and in this way be building up a more and more precise picture of each child's hearing capacity.

The Ewings [58] emphasize the importance of hearing tests. "Without systematic tests there can be no guarantee of any measure of efficiency in procedures designed to help individual children, who are deaf, to enjoy . . . the least imperfect experience of hearing that their residual capacity to hear permits."

There is considerable merit in one teacher's being responsible for all the pure tone and speech testing. This standardises procedures and the results can be compared between any two children throughout the school. Whilst this provides very useful reference data, there is a strong argument for class teachers doing much of their own *speech* testing. The harassed teacher who said "We're here to teach 'em, not to test 'em," had become a victim of a too rigorous application of evaluative techniques. Testing for testings' sake is never, of course, intended, but the most effective method for teachers to obtain the information they require about each child's capacity to hear is by their own careful individual testing (out of school time!).

How Frequently Should Hearing Tests be Given in Schools and Classes for Deaf Children?

There seems to be no hard and fast ruling here, though most would agree that audiograms should be taken at least once each

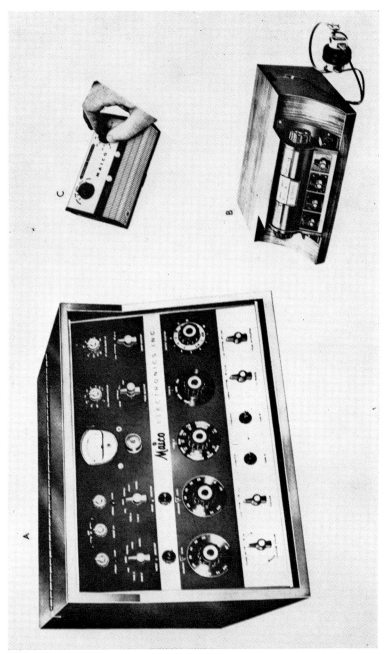

Figure 10. Audiometers of various types.

year. If any medical attention is given tests are made much more frequently than this.

Hearing for speech tests should be made at the same time as audiograms are taken, and at other times as the class teacher sees fit.

PURE TONE TESTS

The Audiometer

The instrument designed to measure human hearing for pure tones is called the *audiometer*. Usually audiometers determine the threshold of audibility of a subject at each octave. The instruments differ widely in shape and in size (Fig. 10), but all have two important controls which are used when a test is administered. The first sets the frequency of the tone to be tested, i.e., whether it is to be high or low in pitch. The second controls the *intensity* or loudness of the sound presented. As a test is made, a graph or *audiogram* is plotted which shows the acuity of a subject's hearing over a range of frequencies (Fig. 11).

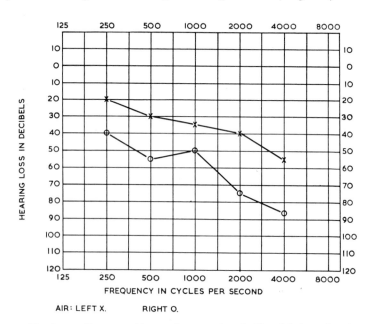

Figure 11. An audiogram. Air conduction thresholds of left and right ears.

In Figure 10, instrument A is a clinical audiometer which is useful to audiologists for administering a variety of diagnostic tests. Audiometer B is a less complicated instrument. It is more portable and has been found useful by specialist teachers travelling to visit children in ordinary schools, i.e., it is sufficiently well equipped to meet the needs of everyday testing situations (e.g., air and bone conduction, masking unit, and speech circuit, etc.). Audiometer C is a *screening audiometer* which has been designed specifically for general practitioners and health nurses. This small, light, battery operated instrument is used to ascertain whether a patient has any significant hearing loss. If such proves to be the case, he is tested at a later date with one of the more versatile audiometers.

"Confusion and disagreement exist as to the preferred method for clinical determination of pure tone thresholds." [21] Carhart and Jerger go on to urge that audiometrists standardise their methods of testing hearing by adopting the basic features of the Hughson-Westlake technique.[99] This "ascending method" involves progressing from a level where the sound is inaudible to the first level where it can be heard, then dropping the intensity by 10 or 15 db., and ascending again.

AIR CONDUCTION TESTING

Children from 3-plus to 7 Years of Age

Steps
1. Check audiometer.
2. Establish rapport.
3. The "Go" game.
4. Pitch pipe as stimulus.
5. Audiometer headset.
6. Begin test at appropriate level and frequency.
7. "Down by tens and up by fives."
8. Record threshold.
9. Test other frequencies.
10. Is masking required?

1. Check the Audiometer. Before the first child of a testing session is asked into the clinic, quickly check your own hearing to ensure the audiometer is working satisfactorily.

2. *Establish Rapport.* Best results are obtained when the child feels happy and confident. Ways which may be used to promote this include:

(a) Helping the mother to relax. It is often quite an ordeal for parents to bring their little children for a first hearing test and they need reassuring just as the child does. If a cup of tea or coffee can be provided for them on arrival at the centre, it frequently does a tremendous amount of good.

(b) To have some coloured play apparatus in your hand when you ask the child into the testing room.

(c) To glance briefly at the child and smile as he enters the clinic.

(d) Smile at the mother also and let her know very briefly what course the session will take, e.g., "I'm just going to give Bobby a few tests, Mrs. Brown, and after that we'll have a good talk about him."

(e) Help the child on to the chair. Such physical contact seems to promote a feeling of security in them.

(f) Let the mother sit near the table if the child seems at all disturbed.

3. *The "Go" Game.* Obtain the child's co-operation in this simple activity.[57] It is often possible to delete a number of the preliminary steps. Instructions which are usually sufficient are as follows:

"Bobby, Mummy (or "Miss Jones"—the assistant) is going to play a little game. When I say "Go!" (or "Now!"), she will take one of these (peg from pegboard) and put it in here," (in a cardboard box lid or in the groove around the edge of the board). "You watch—Go!—Go!" etc. The child is encouraged to watch the tester's face as he or she says the word. After three or four pegs have been moved, say "Now could you do that?" (For young children or those who seem unlikely to co-operate readily, a beat on a drum or chime bar should be used as the initial stimulus, and introduce "Go" or "Now" later.)

4. *Pitch Pipe as Stimulus.* After several successful moves, say "That's good. Now watch Mummy (Miss Jones) play another

game." Use a 1,000 c.p.s. pitch pipe instead of saying "Go." (For children suspected of being very deaf, use a 500 c.p.s. pipe.) Blow the pitch pipe near the child so that he has a good opportunity of hearing it as well as seeing it blown.

When three or four trials have been completed, move behind the mother or the assistant and show that she can do the test without watching the tester. Vary the pauses between signals a little. "Now can you do that?"

5. *Audiometer Headset.* Place the headset of the audiometer on the assistant (or on yourself). Remember to smile as you do this since some children feel nervous at the sight of any such equipment. "Miss Jones is (or I am) going to listen to some more of those little whistles." Point to one ear phone and wait for a moment with a look of concentration on the face—suddenly smile and say "There's one," and move a peg in the peg board. Repeat this several times.

Next place the headset on the child. If he seems worried, it is a good idea to let Mother listen first. (Very occasionally, some children are particularly nervous. With these, one can sometimes remove one receiver from the headset and hold it first against one's own ear, then to the mother's, and finally to the child's. In this way an approximate threshold can be obtained over a limited range of frequencies. Such children are usually very much more co-operative on a second test.)

6. *The First Tone.* The aim is to present a tone to the child which he can hear clearly and yet which is near his threshold and not so loud that it will disturb him. Begin the test at 1,000 c.p.s. at 40 db., if the hearing is likely to be normal and at 70 db., if there seems to be some hearing loss. If the child appears to be very deaf, begin the test at 500 c.p.s. at a level of 70 db. The signal should be not less than one second and not more than two seconds in duration.

7. *"Down by Tens and Up by Fives."* If a response is obtained, drop 10 db., and test again. Quickly reduce the loudness in 10 db. steps until the child fails to respond, then increase in 5 db. steps. On obtaining another response, drop down 10 db., and test up again in fives. The threshold for any frequency is the lowest level at which the child responds three times.

8. *Recording Thresholds.* The conventional symbols are "x" for the left ear and "o" for the right, the frequencies being joined by straight continuous lines.

Provided the audiogram used is a reasonable size, it is fairly general practice to record thresholds for both ears by air and bone conduction, on the one graph. No confusion results when one has become familiar with interpreting such audiograms, and comparisons between ears and between air and bone conduction curves are much easier. There is no necessity to use different colours for recording thresholds, nor to use an audiogram for each ear as is occasionally done.

9. *Test Other Frequencies.* There seems to be no definite ruling about the order in which the other frequencies are tested. One method is to continue from 1,000 to 2,000, and 4,000 and then to go back to 250 and 500. There is little virtue in testing above 4,000 c.p.s. and one can cause fatigue in the child by prolonging the test unnecessarily. If a child is proving difficult to test, try to get an estimate of the hearing loss at 500, 1,000 and 2,000 only—particularly 1,000 c.p.s.

10. *Masking.* Finally, consider the curves obtained for both ears and ask yourself if masking need be applied.

Children Over 7 Years of Age

With older children the approach is similar but it is not necessary to spend so much time in conditioning the child, nor in asking them to shift pegs or blocks, etc., when they hear a sound.

Instructions. "Jean, you are going to hear some whistles like this – – – –." Blow 1,000 c.p.s. or 500 c.p.s. pitch pipe. "When you hear it, will you tap on the table with this pencil?" (Or alternatively, "will you raise your hand?") Demonstrate whichever response you require.

Try first with the child watching and listening and then when listening alone (behind the subject but near the ear).

"Now you are going to hear the same whistles through these," (place the audiometer headset on the child and test as for younger children).

It is usual to test the better ear first and most children from seven or eight years of age can tell you which this is.

BONE CONDUCTION TESTING

Pure tone bone conduction tests are similar in administration to the air conduction tests just described. The following points should, however, be borne in mind:

1. The preliminary "conditioning" period ("Go" game, etc.) can be omitted since bone conduction tests follow air conduction ones in the clinical session.

2. The bone conduction receiver must be very carefully placed on the mastoid process behind the ear. Ensure that there is no hair under the receiver, and that the head band is comfortable.

3. The audiometer is switched to bone conduction!

4. Only three frequencies should be tested—500, 1,000 and 2,000 c.p.s.

5. Any responses in excess of 60 db. should be disregarded.

6. When testing by bone conduction at 55 or 60 db. one must be careful that the signal presented has not been felt as a vibration, rather than heard.

7. Bone conduction tests are not regarded as being as reliable as air conduction ones.

8. Masking should be applied to the ear not being tested.

Masking

When the air conduction threshold in one ear is much better than in the other, it is often necessary to use *masking*. The audiogram shown in Figure 12 is such a case, and it can be seen that the thresholds for the left ear run fairly parallel to those of the right.

It could well be that the hearing loss in the left ear is very much more pronounced than it appears, i.e., that the threshold shown is a spurious one. Sounds, when presented loudly enough to the left ear, are heard in the right one. This occurs for all frequencies, and what is sometimes called a "shadow" audiogram is obtained.

If to the better ear (the right in this case), we apply a fairly loud continuous sound, and at the same time retest the worse ear, it is possible to obtain the true threshold.

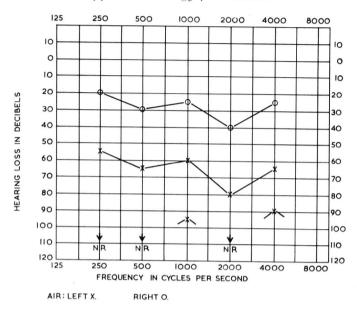

Figure 12. An audiogram showing the effect of masking the better ear.

It is important always to bear in mind that masking may be necessary. In the case cited above (Fig. 12) for example, one might have been tempted to fit the worse ear with a hearing aid.

Masking noises are of two types: *white noise*, and *pure tone*. Just as white light is composed of all the colours in the spectrum, so white noise is a multi-frequency sound. It sounds like, and is sometimes described as, a "frying noise." It is extremely useful when masking sounds of 1,000 c.p.s., or higher. For sounds below 1,000 c.p.s., pure tone or 50 c.p.s. band width masking is more effective. One should use a slightly lower frequency signal than that of the tone being tested. The reason being that the most effective masking is achieved slightly *above* the frequency masked.

Masking should be applied to the better ear if the difference between the ears at any frequency is greater than 35 db. by air conduction and on every occasion when using bone conduction.

Over Masking. It is necessary to guard against over masking. If in the case shown in Fig. 12, for example, 90 db. of masking had been applied to the better ear, the patient would not have been able to hear sounds in either ear.

SPEECH TESTS OF HEARING

It is not proposed here to review the development of all speech tests of hearing. This has been done adequately by Watson and Tolan,[190] Hirsh,[89] Palva,[157] Harold,[86] and others. An attempt will, however, be made to classify most of the speech tests according to difficulty and suitability for deaf children.

The most exacting speech hearing tests have proved to be the nonsense syllable type comprising consonant-vowel-consonant (e.g., wez, nad, gol, etc.), because in such tests it is almost essential to hear every sound in order to obtain maximum score (Fletcher).[62] Lists of monosyllabic words with adult vocabulary have been found easier than nonsense syllables. Due to the limited number of possible combinations of sounds, a subject can frequently hazard a reasonable guess at the word said although he has heard only two of the three phonemes which comprise it. Such tests were constructed by Fry and Kerridge,[71] and at Harvard in 1944 by Hudgins *et al.* (Egan).[42] An even less discriminating test is that of disyllabic words such as those devised by Hudgins *et al.*[97] and those constructed at the Central Institute for the Deaf (Hirsh).[89] Hirsh pointed out that since not all combinations of two syllables constituted words in English, the field of possible responses was further restricted. Finally, for subjects with normal vocabularies, sentence tests are probably the easiest of all the pure auditory discrimination speech tests. It will be appreciated that a listener can supply from the context not only phonemes, but also whole words which have been heard imperfectly. Fletcher and Steinberg[64] used lists of questions to which patients were required to give an answer. Hudgins *et al.*[97] devised easier tests by requiring the listener simply to repeat the question. Fry and Kerridge[71] developed five sentence tests comprising statements rather than questions.

Because of the limited vocabularies of the majority of children with impaired hearing, none of the above tests can be recommended for use in schools for the deaf or in audiology clinics. In spite of this, it was a surprisingly long time before speech tests for such children were published. Numbers and Hudgins[154] adapted the Harvard lists for use in an American school for the deaf. In 1953, T. J. Watson[193] constructed his

M/J lists of monosyllabic words which were taken from the vocabularies of five-year-old Scottish children with normal hearing.
He standardised them for use with English partially deaf children. Watson also modified the Fry-Kerridge lists of sentences for
use with children whose vocabularies were limited.

In spite of the simplified vocabularies of Hudgins' and Watson's tests, they found that they were too difficult for a large
number of the more severely deaf children. Consequently,
Quick,[163] under the direction of Hudgins, constructed a simplified
multiple choice type test which was administered with listening
plus lip-reading. Watson [193] compiled an easier test in which the
child was presented with a set of twenty cards on each of which
six pictures were pasted. The names were printed under each
picture. One word on each card was from the test list. The child
was required to point to one picture in response to the stimulus
he heard. Dalziel [27] reported the use of these lists. The Commonwealth Acoustic Laboratories of Australia developed a similar
test (Murray [148]), which consisted of twenty-five words on each
of five cards. Ten words were tested from each group. This test
could be more quickly administered than Watson's [193] test, although, of course, a certain amount of accuracy was lost. Reed [164]
constructed a similar very useful screening test for use with children from about the age of seven years (Appendix 1). Four pictures of monosyllabic words containing the same vowel (e.g., fish,
dish, pig, ship) are set out on each page of an eight-page booklet
and the child (or adult) is required to discriminate between them
when the four words are said in random order, following the carrier phrase "Show me the——" Kendall [119] developed simple tests
for young deaf children using sets of toys. These lists originally
contained ten test words and two distractors. After naming the
twelve objects as they were taken from the box, the child was
asked to "Put the . . . in the box," or to "Show me the . . . ." Harold [86] adapted Watson's M/J lists (Appendix 2) so that they could
be used for children with more severe impairments of hearing
than had originally been intended. He placed ten words (and
where possible pictures) on each card, five from one list and five
from another. When testing, all five from one test were called and
the five remaining words served as "dummies" or distractors.

None of the pure speech tests described above are satisfactory for the deafest children in schools and classes for deaf children. In consequence, a further test was constructed by the writer.[26] This consisted of discriminating between vowel sounds which were grouped in pairs.

The Paired Vowel Test (Appendix 3) consists of ten pairs of long and short vowels containing similar and dissimilar formant spectra (Miller [140]). The subject is asked to make six discriminations between each two sounds before passing on to the next pair.

It is not for a moment suggested that this simple test is as accurate as the speech tests mentioned above. By using it, however, one is able to ascertain whether a profoundly deaf child has considerable or negligible discrimination for speech sounds. No other tests seem to have been constructed to do this, and it is felt that for this reason too many teachers, doctors and parents, after attempting to administer a speech test which is too difficult for the child, say that a hearing aid will be of no use. Of twenty children tested with hearing losses in excess of 100 db., however, seventeen were found to be able to discriminate accurately between three or more pairs of vowels.[26]

ADMINISTRATION OF SPEECH TESTS

The following speech tests are recommended for children of different ages and different degrees of deafness:

Children Aged Between 7 and 12 Years

1. *Reed's R.N.I.D. Hearing Test Cards.* Administrative instructions are included. Especially useful to doctors, public health nurses and teachers for screening the hearing of children suspected of deafness (Appendix 1).

2. *M/J Words* (Appendix 2). For children whose speech is quite intelligible. Very useful in audiology clinics.

Test 1. Instructions

(Given in a clear deliberate voice—the child watching the speaker.)

"I am going to read you some words and I want you to say the same word that I say—so if I say 'boat,' I want you to say 'boat,' if I say 'three,' I want you to say 'three,' and if I say 'horse,' what would you say?" Give one or two more examples.

"Are you ready?" Read List 1, while the child watches and listens at the same time. If he has a hearing aid he should wear it on the front of the chest. (After you have checked that it is working!) If an error is made by the child, or a word is not said at all, don't repeat it—go on to the next one. Note any errors. If the first ten words are said correctly, go on to Test 2.

Test 2. Instructions

"Now I am going to say some more words, but this time you will not be able to watch my face." Tester stands to one side, and slightly behind the child at a distance of three to four feet. List 2 is then read with the voice kept at a normal conversational level. If this is completed satisfactorily, go on to Test 3 or Test 4.

Test 3.

(If the child has a hearing aid.)

Move in front of him again and say, "Now can you do the same but without your hearing aid?" Remove the aid, and stand three to four feet from the ear in which he has been wearing it. Read List 3.

Test 4.

Move in front of the child again to give the instructions. "This time I am going to *whisper* the words so you will have to listen very carefully." Stand at the side and read List 3. (Be careful to whisper softly!)

Interpreting Results

(a) Teachers in Ordinary Schools: If a child scores 20 or less on Test 1 or Test 2, the principal of the school should inform the Medical Officer of Health.

If a child appears to have a very slight deafness (say, five or less errors in Test 3), it is worthwhile to re-check the hearing again in a week's time, so that the medical people are not notified unnecessarily. If you are at all doubtful, however, the child should be referred.

(b) *Clinic Workers and Teachers of Deaf Children:* The speech test results should confirm the threshold obtained in the air conduction audiometric test.

As mentioned earlier, it is often possible to obtain scores when the child is tested with and without the hearing aid, which convince children that the aid *is* of benefit to them. It is not uncommon, for example, to obtain a percentage of eighty, aided, and perhaps twenty-four unaided (score in 25 words × 4).* It is relatively easy then to point out to the child that the aid should be worn regularly.

3. *Adapted M/J Words.* For children with defective speech and whose hearing losses do not exceed 90 db.

Lists in book form (see Fig. 13), ten words per page for the first five pages, five words from List 1 and five from List 2. Next five pages compiled from Lists 3 and 4, and so on.

Test 1. Subject reads words on one page, and then watches and listens (with his hearing aid, or the audiometer headset), as words from List 1 are delivered. Child points to the word he thinks was said. All of List 1 is read, the words of List 2 acting as distractors.

Test 2. "Now can you do that without looking at me?" Read List 3—being careful to give the child time to read the ten words on each page before the five being tested are delivered.

Test 3. With some children it will be possible to administer this test without the hearing aid—use List 5.

It is possible, with this test, to give a series of lists at different loudness levels and by comparing the scores obtained, to establish the best listening level for a particular child. It would be advisable to do this in those cases where the child chooses a level which seems very different from that suggested by Harold [86] for a child with his pure tone threshold.

4. *Paired Vowel Test* (Appendix 3). Generally for children whose hearing losses exceed 100 db.

Using the practice pair (ee, ir), the tester says the sounds carefully three or four times close to the hearing aid, while the child listens and watches. The children at this stage often think

---

* A difference of four words (i.e., 16%) is necessary before differences between lists of twenty-five words are statistically significant.

they are to have a speech lesson, so begin to repeat the sounds as they are said. If they have difficulty understanding that it is a listening test and not a speaking one, the tester can usually make it clear by gently pressing the child's lips together while saying, "Don't you speak, just listen," and tapping the hearing aid receiver. The tester says "Which one is ee?" and the child points to it. The sounds are then said in random order while the child points to them.

The test is repeated when the child is listening alone.

The test then begins with the first pair "ar, oo," which are indicated by the tester four times as the tester says each sound. The sounds are then given individually, e.g., "ar, oo, oo, ar, ar, oo." As soon as the child makes an error, stop the test and give him an opportunity to hear the pair again. If a second mistake is made, discontinue testing that pair and go on to the next. If there were no errors in the six trials, score two points. If there was one error score one point, and more than one error, score no points.

When the ten pairs have been tested, multiply the scores by five to obtain a percentage correct. If 30 per cent or more is obtained, it is felt that a hearing aid is likely to be well worthwhile.

Speech Tests for Children Aged 12-plus

(a) For Children Whose Speech is Intelligible: The words contained in the M/J lists are too easy for older children, i.e., the scores obtained are much higher than is reasonable if they are used with children from about twelve years of age. In consequence, the Commonwealth Acoustic Laboratories' adaptation of the MRC Word Lists are recommended (Appendix 4). These lists are administered in just the same way as the M/J lists described above.

(b) For Older Children Who are Severely and Profoundly Deaf, the adapted M/J words and the Paired Vowel Discrimination Test may be used.

Speech Tests for Young Children

1. Kendall's [120] *Toy Test (K/T).* For children with some vocabulary and a hearing loss not greater than about 85 db.

Kendall described a speech test which he devised for young

deaf children. These tests have been used in the Department of Audiology and Education of the Deaf at The University of Manchester, and elsewhere, for a number of years, and are an extremely useful test for the teacher or the clinician.

Five lists, each of twelve paired monosyllabic nouns, were chosen (Appendix 5), and the lists were equated for difficulty.

In administration, twelve toys, representing each twelve words, are placed in a box. The tester removes the first object, asking, "What's the name of that?"—"That's right. That's the horse—or spoon—or brush, etc." When all the objects have been named by the child, and spread in front of him, he is required to replace them in the box one by one when asked to do so. "Put the shoe in the box," "Put the key in the box," etc.

It can be seen that as the test progresses, the number of objects on the table is reduced, so that the child is discriminating between fewer and fewer possible words, i.e., the test is becoming easier and easier. To counteract this a little, only the first ten words in each list are used in the test—the last two words being included as distractors.

It is sometimes possible to ask the child to "Show me the — —," rather than to put it in the box, and in this way to keep the test of equal difficulty throughout. For the younger children, however, this never seems so successful as does the activity of putting the toys away.

The tester must decide under what conditions this test is to be administered, depending on the apparent defect of the child. If the hearing loss appears to be very slight, the first list could be delivered at a conversational level—60-70 db., and a second list whispered at 40-45 db.

If there seems to be a hearing loss greater than 30 db., and less than 90 db., the first list may be given with the child watching and listening at one of the three levels recommended by Harold.*

The second test (List 2) could be given with the child listen-

---

* Hearing loss . . . . suggested listening level.
30 - 50 db. . . . . 80 db. above normal threshold of detectability.
50 - 75 db. . . . . 90 db. above normal threshold.
75 - 90 db. . . . . 100 db. above normal threshold.

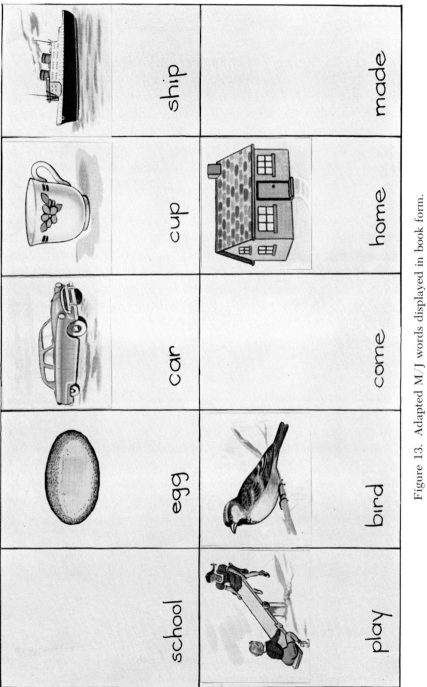

Figure 13. Adapted M/J words displayed in book form.

ing without watching, and if this is successfully completed the level may be reduced in the successive tests until the child has difficulty in performing the test.

If a mistake is made by the child, e.g., he puts the "cow" in the box when the word "house" was said, mark "house" as an error, and continue reading the list, omitting the word "cow" when it comes, of course. Say, "Put the 'house' in the box" again at the end, but do not mark it as correct. Finally, put the toys out again and say, "Put the 'cow' in the box," (and any other words which have not so far been read). The number of words out of ten which were heard correctly are multiplied by ten to obtain the percentage.

This is a very useful test for school nurses, visiting teachers, doctors, etc., when wanting to screen the hearing of children in their first two years at school. It is attractive to little children, and the fact that the child is not required to speak, but simply to move an object, makes it easy for shy children.

2. *Improvised Toy Test*

For very deaf young children, or those with very restricted vocabularies, the K/T tests above are too difficult. It is necessary here to choose words which are known to the child, and often to reduce the number of items used. Such modifications necessarily render the test less accurate, and they can at best be regarded as a crude estimate of a child's hearing for speech. They are useful, nevertheless, if carefully administered.

When making up such a test, choose words which are known to the child, and as far as possible have dissimilar vowels, e.g., boat, horse, car, tree, dog, might be a suitable little list.

3. *Paired Vowel Test*

For pre-school children with hearing losses in excess of 100 db.

It is possible to teach quite young children to perform the paired vowel test after a little practice—work from the "Go game" technique. Teachers in nursery schools and classes have a good opportunity to do this if they are able to do a little individual work with their children every day. Instead of vowel sounds, e.g., "ar" and "oo," discriminations can be made between words using these same vowels—"car" and "spoon."

CLINICAL AUDIOMETRY

There are six steps in a normal clinical session for children from about the age of three and a half years:

(1) Careful study of any case notes available.
(2) Pure tone air conduction tests.
(3) Speech tests.
(4) Bone conduction tests.
(5) Discussion with parents.
(6) Diagnosis and recommendation.

Case Notes

Letters of referral are sometimes not very helpful. "Would you please see this child with regards deafness?" is often all that the letter contains. Before a child comes to an audiology clinic, however, it is usually very useful to know certain things about him. How old is he? Is his home a "good" one? Has he been tested before? If so, what were the results? If he is at school, what does his headmaster say of his attainments and general adjustment? What special facilities are available in his area?

If you have been given no indication of how deaf the child is, you may be inclined to ask the mother as soon as she enters the clinic—"Do you think John is very deaf?" or "Well, what do you think is the problem?" The only snag in so doing, is that many mothers once started are sometimes difficult to stop! Quite understandably, they are often very worried about their child and are keen to tell all they know. It is most important that they be given the opportunity to do this before the end of the session. It is important also, however, that one gets on as quickly as is possible with the testing. The child can become bored with sitting doing nothing and may start exploring the clinic, or may become nervous and unable to co-operate in the tests when he is finally asked to do so. For these reasons some testers prefer to ask no questions at all at the beginning of a session, others are more specific in their questioning, e.g., "Do you think John has a severe or a slight hearing problem?"

Pure Tone Air Conduction Tests

With experience, one should be able to move quickly and smoothly through the steps which lead up to the audiometric test. It is important that time is not wasted on these preliminaries so that the child begins the test with a minimum of fatigue.

Points to watch when administering an audiometric test include:

(a) The length of the stimulus sound. The signal should be presented for approximately two seconds. If they are of shorter duration than this, particularly when nearing threshold, they can be ignored by the child. They should not be continued too long, and if the subject begins to move a peg in the pegboard, or to tap the table before the two seconds is up, the tester should discontinue the signal.

(b) The time between any two signals should be varied occasionally, but it can be quite short.

(c) With little children, a change of activity is often useful in maintaining interest, e.g., they can take the pegs from the pegboard, next build and take down a tower of locking blocks, then make a pyramid from plastic rings etc., and finally replace the pegs in the board.

Speech Tests of Hearing

(a) In administering speech tests, always work from the most easy condition to the more difficult. For example, severely deaf children should look and listen with aided hearing first, then with aided hearing only, and finally with unaided hearing alone. In this way, they feel much more confident than if asked to do the most difficult test first. Similarly children who appear to be only slightly deaf should be given their first speech test at say 80 db., and then the speech should be reduced to quieter levels.

(b) The speech should be monitored either by using the speech circuit of an audiometer or speech training aid, or by means of a sound level meter if the tests are made free field.

It is most important in the latter case to ensure that the sound level meter is placed in the correct position before the test is begun (Fig. 14). The microphone of the meter should be the

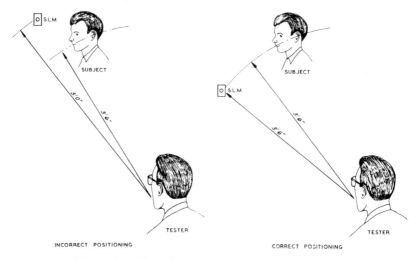

Figure 14. The placing of the sound level meter.

same distance from the speaker as is the ear of the subject being tested. This may be achieved by the tester or a colleague holding the meter, or by the child holding it.

(c) Recorded or live voice? For older children and adults, recorded lists of words are very useful and are more scientific than live voice tests. Identical test conditions can of course be obtained more nearly by using recorded material than is possible when lists are read by the tester each time—no matter how skilful he or she may be.

Despite this, live voice tests, provided they are well administered, have very many advantages. They are more personal than are recorded tests. The tester can thus deliver a word at precisely the time that seems most suitable to the child, e.g., there is less likelihood of a child having to wait for a word or of receiving a word before he is ready for it. Some children respond quite quickly to the test words, others, particularly cerebral palsied children for example, require much more time to reply or to identify the word said. A test which is found to be too easy or too difficult can be discontinued at any point and a more suitable test administered without delay—with recorded material difficulty is sometimes experienced in finding the exact place required on the tape or the disc—and if this is not so, the technique is necessarily more time consuming than when live voice is used.

In my own experience live voice testing has proved very satisfactory in speech reception tests.

Bone Conduction Tests

(a) There is no hard and fast rule about the order in which speech tests and bone conduction tests should be administered. If a child has tested quickly and reliably by air conduction, one can frequently go straight on to test by bone conduction. If, however, the air conduction test has been somewhat prolonged, and there have been signs of fatigue, it is often advisable to insert the speech tests to give the child a break from that type of activity.

(b) It is usually a good idea to tell the child, "This test won't take long."

Discussion With the Parents

By the time the tester is ready to make a diagnosis and a recommendation he has usually built up a fairly accurate estimate of the child's ability to hear. As one becomes familiar with deafness and the handicap which varying degrees of it impose on children, one is able to estimate with fair accuracy what the effect of a given impairment will be. When this is considered in relation to the other known factors of intelligence, home background, special services available, it is usually possible to suggest what type of educational therapy is likely to produce the best results.

In diagnosis, one problem when speaking or writing to speech therapists, doctors, etc., is to find a satisfactory means of describing the hearing loss. To say for example that a child "has an auditory impairment in his left ear of 65 db.," means almost nothing to the majority of laymen. For this reason, such terms as "slight but not significant hearing loss," "slight but significant . . . ," "partial hearing," "severe deafness," and "profound deafness" are often useful. As a rule, however, they require some amplification and the best way to do this seems to be with examples of what the children can or cannot hear; e.g., a child with a hearing loss of 80 db. might be described as "a severely deaf child—she hears next to nothing of speech when it is at an ordinary conversational level; when using a hearing aid, however, she is able to hear 50 per cent of simple speech material (single words) correctly. . . ." Again a child whose hearing loss is in excess of 100 db. could perhaps be described as "a profoundly deaf child—she is able to hear voice but only when it is made at the level of a loud shout very close to the ear;" and so on.

Recommendations

Unless you are a doctor or an otologist, it is advisable to preface every recommendation with "If nothing can be done to improve this hearing loss, . . ." (If writing to the family doctor or to an otologist, the phrasing might be "If this impairment proves irreversible . . .".) It should be emphasised that although an audiologist is justified and indeed is expected to diagnose the extent of a person's deafness on a given day, he is not qualified to make any suggestions about causation or even whether the deafness appears to be conductive, perceptive or mixed in origin. (Although, of course, through the shape and the relationship of the air and bone conduction thresholds, one frequently has a fair idea.)

Chapter 3

THE EXTENT OF THE HEARING LOSS

THE PURE TONE AUDIOGRAM AND HEARING FOR SPEECH

THE RELATIONSHIP BETWEEN the pure tone audiogram and hearing for speech has received the attention of a large number of workers. To mention one or two, Carhart [14] gave hearing tests to 682 persons with varying types of deafness and found that he was better able to predict the hearing loss for speech by averaging the hearing losses at 512, 1024 and 2048 c.p.s. than from seven other methods of calculation, from the pure tone audiogram. A more complicated method was evolved by Fletcher [63] based on a table of loudness which included the relative contributions especially to intelligibility of various frequency bands. He also gave a simplified method of calculation which consisted of averaging the two smallest losses for the three tones 512, 1000 and 2000 c.p.s. He considered this method almost as accurate as the first. Palva [157] evaluated the various methods of estimating hearing loss for speech from the pure tone audiogram and concluded that the method prepared by Carhart proved most reliable. This method of calculation seems fairly generally accepted in most countries at the present time.

Juers,[116] like Cawthorn and Harvey,[23] believed that the correlation between the audiogram and hearing loss for speech was very close in conductive deafness, but that it was not so close for other types. There seems to be considerable agreement that what each patient will hear of speech can not be predicted accurately from the audiogram in nerve deafened cases. Ewing [46] pointed out that hearing for conversational speech could not be predicted from threshold data. Palva [157] found that nerve deafened cases with average hearing losses between 20 and 40 db. had speech discrimination losses which varied between 10 and 30 per cent. Siegenthaler and Gunn,[172] after examining one hundred cases

47

with nerve deafness, concluded that prediction from audiograms alone should not be made.

The *aetiology* (cause of deafness) in nerve deafened cases had some bearing on auditory discrimination according to Cawthorn and Harvey.[23] Harold[86] found that a group of twenty measles cases heard rather better than did children whose deafness resulted from one of eight other causes, and that six cerebral palsy cases heard significantly worse than did the other eight groups.

The shape of the audiogram is considered by many workers to be important in determining whether a subject will hear well or not. Huizing,[102] Wedenberg,[197] Getz[74] and others contended that flat audiograms (those with approximately equal losses for all frequencies) are better from this point of view than are those which possess a downward slope for the higher frequencies. Harold,[86] however, found little relationship between audiogram shape and hearing for speech.

The presence or absence of a phenomenon known as *loudness recruitment* in subjects has been found by various workers to have some effect on the extent to which they are able to hear speech. Where recruitment is present, a deaf person is able to hear loud sounds as loudly (or almost as loudly) as does a person with normal hearing. A considerable body of literature exists on this subject and will be discussed later.

When to the above factors are added others such as intelligence, age, language background, familiarity with the test situation, and the degree of rapport established between child and tester, as well as a few others, it is easy to understand how two children may have identical audiograms, yet may obtain quite different scores on word list tests.

It is possible, however, to look at an audiogram and make some general statements about what the particular patient is *likely* to hear, after one becomes familiar with audiograms and their interpretation. Figure 15 represents the better ear thresholds of nine hypothetical cases all of whom may be said to have *perceptive* or *nerve* deafnesses. Before commenting briefly on these, it is stressed again that audiograms should never really be

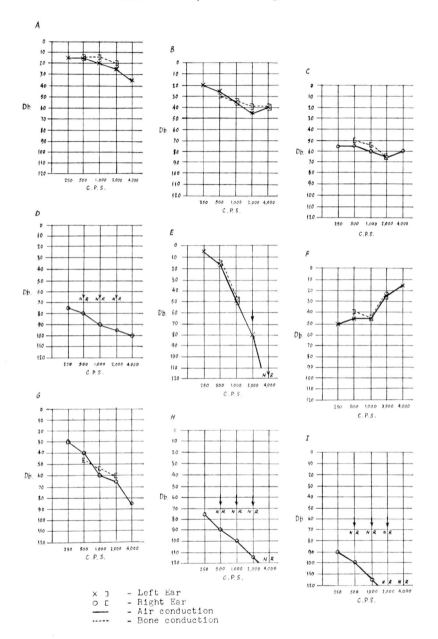

Figure 15. Better ear thresholds of nine cases.

interpreted in isolation—pure tone and speech tests of hearing form the basis of clinical audiometry.

Audiogram A (Hearing Loss 20 db.). This child is not sufficiently deaf to wear a hearing aid,* but does have an annoying little hearing loss. Other things being equal, such a child might be expected to be coping satisfactorily in an ordinary school while sitting in the front of the class. The teacher should know about her disability. In particular this will ensure that the child is not penalised for behaviour which may seem like lack of attention or disobedience but which in fact may well be the result of not having heard or of having heard imperfectly. It is unlikely that her speech will have been adversely affected by such a hearing loss.

Audiogram B (Hearing Loss 35 db.). A child whose hearing in the better ear is represented in Audiogram B has a significant hearing loss, but with a hearing aid in good acoustic conditions many such children are able to hear simple word list material with 100 per cent accuracy. Unaided, this child could be expected to hear the vowels of conversational speech fairly adequately, but some of the consonants would be heard imperfectly and in some cases not at all. In consequence of this, if the loss is of long standing, and the child has not used a hearing aid regularly, his production of some consonants might well be defective. When watching the speaker such children can understand running speech quite well unaided.

The majority of children with hearing losses of this order seem to cope well in ordinary schools when hearing aids are worn properly. Many such children dislike having to wear hearing aids. "I can hear as well without it," they frequently say. They *do* need aids, however, and should be persuaded to wear them in school at least. Some require speech therapy to help them articulate consonants clearly.

Audiogram C (Hearing Loss 60 db.). This audiogram represents a more serious hearing loss. If listening unaided a child with such an audiogram would hear very little of the sounds of

---

* Hearing aids are not normally recommended unless the hearing loss by air conduction in the better ear is at least 30 db. and this loss is irreversible.

ordinary conversational speech. The child's own speech will be grossly defective unless he has been given special help. Despite this, a flattish audiogram at about this level is regarded by many audiologists as a "good" one, since very often such cases hear well with amplification. It is not uncommon for such a case as this to obtain a score of 70 per cent correct in a word list test when listening with his hearing aid and without watching the speaker, providing the acoustic conditions are good. If such children are of reasonable intelligence and have a good home as well as an understanding teacher, some are able to manage in ordinary schoolrooms. Many, however, require special educational treatment in classes for partially hearing children.

Audiogram D (Hearing Loss 88 db.). A child with this audiogram is very severely deaf. Many such children hear a great deal of speech when it is amplified, and using a simplified word list test (to be described later), some of these children are able to obtain scores of 40 and even 50 per cent when listening alone.

Audiogram E (Hearing Loss 48 db.—Steeply sloping). Hearing losses of this type appear from time to time. Very often deafness is not suspected for a long time because such children are able to respond to very quiet sound provided it is of low frequency. They may hear a car or an airplane when it is a long way off simply because there is enough sound of low frequency to become audible to them. Similarly the *fundamental pitch* of a speaker's voice will be audible to them, so that often when their name is called quite softly, they will turn in the direction of the speaker. Parents, teachers and doctors then frequently think, "Oh well, whatever else is wrong with young Billy, at least he's not deaf." Unfortunately their retarded speech development and their failure to establish normal relations with their peers often lead to diagnoses of "innate dullness," or perhaps of "brain damage," "aphasia" or "auditory imperception." In fact, such children are simply very deaf over most of the speech range of frequencies and of course for sounds above these.

Hearing aids are usually of little benefit to them—any amplification of the lower frequencies makes those sounds unpleasantly loud, and the hearing mechanism is so defective for the higher frequencies, that intelligibility is rarely attainable. The majority of such children require regular special educational treatment. They then obtain a clear speech pattern to lipread and are able to be given constant help with their speech. They hear the melody of music very clearly but are not able to understand the words of songs—speech often being heard rather like a succession of "oo" sounds.

Audiogram F (Hearing Loss 38 db.). Very occasionally, a child is found to have better hearing for high frequencies than for low ones. Such children often hear speech well when it is aided, and consonants, not surprisingly, are heard particularly clearly. Unaided speech to such cases lacks body and this is sometimes reflected in their own speaking voices.

Audiogram G (Hearing Loss 55 db.). This is quite a common audiogram for nerve deafened cases, i.e., hearing is frequently worse for high frequencies than for the lower ones. Voice quality is often quite good in such cases, due to the fact that a useful amount of the vowel sounds can be heard when a hearing aid is used and pitch and rhythm are able to be perceived and incorporated into the child's speech.

Audiogram H (Hearing Loss 102 db.). Although profoundly deaf, many children with audiograms such as this, show fair discrimination between known words or vowels. Usually they are able to discriminate pitch and rhythm from music when it is amplified. Unless given a great deal of speech therapy by skilled teachers such children frequently develop speech which is not intelligible to untrained listeners.

Audiogram I (Hearing Loss 112 db. [Approximately]). Despite very little hearing for speech or any other sound, many such cases are able to discriminate between some pairs of vowels when they are presented in random order. Van Uden has found that it is possible for even such deaf children as this to perceive music and derive pleasure from dancing and from listening to music.

Profoundly deaf people will never hear speech as clearly as those who are only partially hearing, no matter how loudly the speech is delivered. Murray [149] put this well when he stated that "the ultimate limitation of hearing aids is not a physical, but a physiological one." In other words, the physicists could give a hearing aid any output and any frequency response which was asked for, but there are people whose organ of hearing is so defective that speech can never be made intelligible to them.

There are, of course, an infinite number of categories of deafness—ranging from losses which are only just significant right through to those where sounds must be presented so loudly that they are almost painful before they can be detected.

The percentage of children who are totally deaf has been found to be very small. Goodman [76] examined all the children between the ages of eight years and twelve years eleven months in seven schools for the deaf in England. In all, 343 children were tested and only 5 per cent were considered totally deaf. Dalziel [27] found 7 per cent of the 1,770 children he tested in schools for the deaf who failed to respond to the sound of voice at 135 db. above .0002 dynes/cm^2. Yenrick [206] found only two children in a deaf school population of four hundred who possessed no measurable hearing, and van Uden [184] only five in a school of two hundred, and these were possible cases of mental deficiency.

Whitehurst [203] made a case study of a girl of six years with a hearing loss of 87 db. (American Standard) who after training was able to discriminate one hundred words by listening alone.

Where the hearing impairment was greatly in excess of 90 db., however, workers found that amplification was not sufficient to enable listeners to obtain intelligible speech reception without also watching the speaker.

The American Medical Association [1] drew up a table for converting audiometric db. losses into percentage of loss for speech. This table showed that they considered a patient with a threshold of 90 db. (American Standard) from 512 to 1024 c/s and of 95 from 1024 to 2048 c/s to have a "total loss of serviceable hearing." Watson [89] regarded the above evaluation by the A.M.A. as somewhat conservative, but he did suggest that it was close to the absolute maximum limits. He claimed that with rare exceptions, patients with losses in excess of 100 db. at 1 Kc and 2 Kc could get no practical intelligibility through the use of even the finest hearing aid. A hearing aid for such a patient could provide "only a partial key to phrasing, rhythm and pitch" (p. 539). Watson recommended that aids should not be fitted for people whose loss at 1 Kc and 2 Kc was greater than 95 db. (American Standard) unless they understood fully "the limited if not doubtful benefit" which they could expect from them. Later Watson (and Tolan)[190] considered that a loss of 100 db. over 1024 and 2048 c.p.s. was the maximum impairment that could be reached by a wearable hearing aid, and the limit was generally 95 db.

At the conclusion of a three year study of the effect of hearing aid use on a deaf school population, Myklebust[151] suggested a numerical classification with implications for the acoustic training at each level. For children with hearing losses up to 95 db. (American Standard), Myklebust suggested the aim should be to develop normal comprehension by hearing, i.e., the acoustic method predominating and all other methods supplemented to this. He noted more variation in the progress of children with losses from 76 to 89 db. Children whose losses ranged between 90 and 94 db., Myklebust regarded as the "borderline acoustic groups"—some responded successfully and some did not. For children with impairments in excess of 95 db. he felt that acoustic training was not indicated except in the rare cases of adventitious deafness where a child had retained the sound pattern after becoming deaf. Forty-eight per cent of the school population fell in the under 90 db. group, 15 per cent in the 90-95 db. group and the remaining 37 per cent had hearing losses greater than 95 db.

Ewing and Ewing[58] after outlining courses for children with differing hearing losses, suggested that for those whose impairments exceeded 95 db., auditory training was likely to be of no benefit and that sight and touch should take the place of hearing.

Silverman[175] as a result of his work on increasing tolerance levels (1947) suggested that some individuals who had previously been termed "totally deaf" might be reached by auditory stimulation through properly designed apparatus.

The deafest children in Hudgins' longitudinal study of the effect of auditory training on the speech perception of thirteen profoundly deaf and four partially deaf children (1954), had hearing losses of 98 db. (American Standard). Hudgins considered it inadvisable to include children whose auditory impairments were greater than this.[96]

The worker who has studied most extensively the use of hearing aids by children whose hearing losses exceed 100 db. is van

Uden. Although it would not be true to say that he believes every profoundly deaf child can benefit from the use of a hearing aid, he certainly has shown that the majority can and that every child should be given a lengthy trial.

My own experience with these deaf children tends to confirm van Uden's findings. If these children can be enabled to hear even a trace of speech—and all but a handful can—then surely it can only be of benefit to them. Even if all the vowels he can hear sound rather like a muffled "oo," the sound of voice must provide a link with the people who speak to him. How important it must be psychologically to a young deaf child, for example, in giving him or her that sense of belonging—the realisation that when his mother speaks, "sound" accompanies the movements of the lips. Van Uden [183] has quoted a girl whose hearing loss was 100 db. and who on removing her hearing aid said, "Now I am alone again." The Ewings have made the good point, too, that even sound imperfectly heard can help a deaf person realise when words begin and end, as this is not always possible by lipreading alone.

Further evidence of the value of sound to a profoundly deaf person is contained in the following case study.

> Mrs. M........
> Aged—Thirty-two years
> Aetiology—Scarlet fever
> Age at onset of deafness—Two years
> Hearing loss—113 db. (approximately)
> A skillful lipreader
> Speech—mostly intelligible but grossly defective

Mrs. M. was fitted with a hearing aid for the first time when thirty-two years of age. After a three-week introductory period consisting of five talks on hearing aids, how they should be worn and cared for, and what benefit might be expected when wearing one, Mrs. M. was issued with her aid. At the end of the first day she reported: "I have had a very interesting day. I heard my children talking for the first time. Their voices sounded high to me compared with Mrs. —— who lives nearby and who seems to have a gruff voice. I heard the cupboard doors click when I shut them, and oh! the noise of the dishes when I was washing up. I also heard the water splashing on the walls of the swimming baths when I was watching the children swimming this afternoon. Do car gears make a noise when you change them?"

For the first two or three weeks Mrs. M. had considerable difficulty with headaches—often immediately after removing the aid. Sometimes wearing the aid made her dizzy, and she often woke with a headache. She found that a cup of tea often dispelled these. On one or two days during this early period Mrs. M. left the aid off completely. She was encouraged to *switch* it off rather than *take* it off when wearing it became unpleasant.

Before the end of one month, Mrs. M. was wearing her aid continuously with no ill effects. During the five months under which she was observed, Mrs. M. reported hearing (imperfectly, of course) a variety of sounds which included: doors shutting, furniture when moved on a hard floor, the vacuum cleaner, her own footsteps, shovelling coke, washing and drying dishes, the piano (sometimes), the dance band and a male soloist at a ball, laughter, a baby crying, children singing at a Girl Guide party, her children if they quarrelled in another room, an ambulance siren and, and people's voices.

Mrs. M. noted that "all people's voices are different." Some ladies' voices she said, were clear and high, some were soft and others were "active" (chatterboxes!). Men spoke with "firm" and "strong" voices. Although being able to detect this pitch and quality in the voices, Mrs. M. was not able, of course, to obtain "intelligibility." She felt, however, that she was able to lip-read better, and the neighbours all told her her speech was more intelligible to them. I, personally, could perceive a slight, but not a striking, improvement in her speech. Mr. M. considered that a most valuable contribution which the hearing aid had made was that his wife had now become accustomed to keeping the level of her voice down, whereas previously he had frequently to remind her to do this.

At the end of the fifth month, Mrs. M. was asked if she thought the hearing aid worthwhile, and to this she replied, "Oh yes, I wouldn't be without it."

Cases such as that cited above are very valuable ones, for three main reasons:

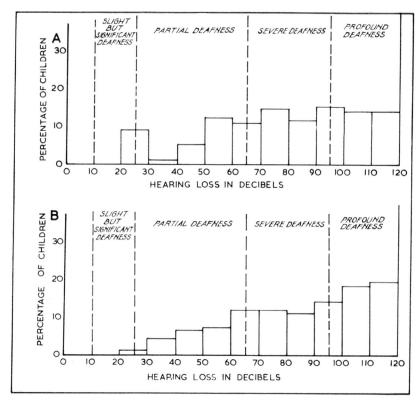

Figure 16. Distribution of children attending schools for the deaf and partially deaf according to hearing loss. A. England (512 12-year-olds), B. New Zealand (307 children).

(a) The majority of deaf people are not as deaf as this (see Fig. 16). It seems reasonable to assume, therefore, that having a less defective hearing organ, most of them should derive *more* benefit from sound than was the case here.

(b) They emphasise that it is not essential to have a hearing aid during the first year or two of life, to derive benefit from it. Older deaf children and adults (as well as some teachers and doctors) frequently use this as an argument for not obtaining hearing aids. Although it is desirable to begin early, it is never too late to make a start.

(c) They emphasise to those of us who work with deaf children that hearing aid users do have problems, particularly those connected with physical discomfort in the early stages and teachers and parents of young children should watch closely for any signs of these.

Not all cases are as successful as that of Mrs. M. and as far as getting male old pupils of schools for the deaf to wear hearing aids is concerned, I have had singularly poor results to date. Factors involved in obtaining the full time use of aids are discussed in some detail in Chapter 8.

The Distribution of Hearing Losses Among Children in Schools for the Deaf and Partially Hearing

Having surveyed very briefly the audiological difficulties which confront deaf people with various hearing losses, it is interesting and relevant here to consider the distribution of hearing losses among the deaf children in special schools. For example, are nearly all the children in the schools profoundly deaf?

Myklebust [151] classified all the children in a large American school for the deaf as follows:

Less than 90 db. hearing loss	48 per cent
90-95 db. hearing loss	15 per cent
Greater than 95 db. hearing loss	37 per cent

By testing all the twelve-year-old children in English schools for the deaf and partially hearing, Murphy [145] considered he had

TABLE 1

Hearing Loss Decibels	Murphy's Sample (512 children) %	New Zealand Schools (307 children) %
20 - 29	9.48	0.98
30 - 39	1.06	3.59
40 - 49	6.64	5.48
50 - 59	11.18	6.84
60 - 69	10.97	11.08
70 - 79	12.25	11.08
80 - 89	10.78	10.11
90 - 99	13.62	12.05
100 - 109 ⎱	24.00	18.24
110 - 119 ⎰		19.91

obtained a representative sample of their total population. In consequence, his data shown in Table 1 are most useful. It has been possible to obtain the hearing losses of all the children attending the three New Zealand schools for the deaf and partially hearing who were able to co-operate in an audiometric test in December, 1959. The figures obtained, together with those of Dr. Murphy, are set out in Table 1 and are graphed in Figure 16.

Histograms A and B in Figure 16 emphasise the fact that there is a tremendous amount of useful hearing amongst the pupils in schools for the deaf. This fact is seldom fully appreciated and is scarcely ever fully exploited. There is a tendency to think of deaf children in two categories only, the partially hearing and the deaf, i.e., the Grade II B children and the Grade III's [9] and with the "partially hearing" group, to recommend the acoustic approach, but with the "deaf" children, to say that one has to rely on other methods. It is, of course, true that some changes in techniques are required when teaching the deafer children, but to ignore the hearing factor with such pupils is making both the child's and the teacher's task unnecessarily more difficult. For those of us who entered this field before audiology had made any appreciable impact on teaching deaf children, it can take some time before one is able to convince oneself of the often critical value of sound to nearly all children in schools for the deaf. The deaf children themselves, by rejecting their hearing aids as they so frequently do if given the opportunity, seem also to be suggesting that aids are of no real benefit.

These and other relevant questions are discussed at some length in Chapter 8, entitled "The Provision of Auditory Experience." In Chapter 2, some tests and procedures have been described which have helped both teachers and children to appreciate the value of hearing aids.

Chapter 4

THE FREQUENCIES AND INTENSITIES OF
SPEECH SOUNDS

In speech training with hearing aids, one should really bear in mind: (a) the audiogram of the child, (b) the frequencies of the speech material being given, and (c) the frequency characteristics and output of the hearing aid being used. The theory does not always work out exactly as it should in practice—children sometimes failing to hear sounds which they *should* be able to hear, and vice versa. The more one knows of the physics of speech, however, the more intelligently one is able to use hearing aids with deaf children and the more interesting does the work become.

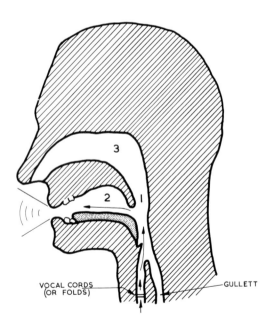

Figure 17. The production of a vowel sound.

THE PRODUCTION OF VOWEL SOUNDS

When the intercostal muscles contract, they pull the ribs out-wards so that a vacuum is created within the cage or box-like structure of the chest. Air is thus sucked into the lungs and may be held there for quite a period if we desire it, simply by closing the little valve in the throat. This valve, located in the larynx and protected in the front by two pieces of cartilage which are pop-ularly known as "the Adam's apple," contains two folds in the wall of the larynx called the *vocal cords* (Fig. 17). When the vocal cords are drawn almost together, the air passing between them sets them in vibration, and a sound results. This sound is called the *fundamental* or *laryngeal* tone. The speed with which the vocal cords vibrate determines the pitch of the voice, and in any speaker (except some very deaf ones), the pitch rises and falls a great deal—as much as 100 cycles in a two-syllable word at times. The pitch of the fundamental ranges from about 90 cycles to 300 cycles. The average pitch of a woman's voice is about 250 cycles—roughly that of middle C on the piano. For men, the average fundamental tone is nearer 125 cycles. When only the edges of the cords are set in vibration, a very high pitched or "falsetto" voice results. When excess pressure is placed on the vocal cords, they are unable to vibrate freely throughout their whole length, and a hoarse, breathy type of speech results.

It is not easy to say exactly what a laryngeal tone would sound like, but it is likely that it would be a fairly indefinite sound such as a prolongation of the central vowel [ə] as in "father." We never hear the pure laryngeal tone, however, since before it reaches us it has passed through and been affected by the re-sonating chambers above, i.e., the naso-pharynx, the mouth cavity and the nose (Fig. 17, 1, 2, and 3 respectively).

As the fundamental tone bounds about in these cavities, it causes them to resonate, before it issues from the lips as the sound we require. Just which frequencies emerge, depends upon the shape of the cavities at that particular time. Little children (with normal hearing) soon learn to modify the shape of their mouths so that the vowel which issues forth, sounds like the one they want to hear. Babies can frequently be heard experimenting with their voices in this way.

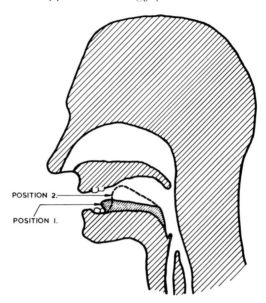

POSITION 2.

POSITION 1.

Figure 18. Change in tongue position—and hence in shape of resonating cavity in the production of the diphthong [aɪ] as in "*tie*."

One does not teach speech to very deaf children for long before one realises that the tongue position is all important in obtaining clear vowels and diphthongs. In the diphthong [aɪ] (as in "tie"), for example, the tongue must be down at the back to give the [a] sound (as in "farm") and must then move quickly forward and upward to the [ɪ] position (as in "see") [Fig. 18, Positions 1 and 2]). It is important to realise that whilst the resonator changes shape and thus alters the sound which comes from the speaker, the fundamental remains the same sound. If, however, a scale is sung using one vowel sound—then the reverse applies. There is no change in the shape of the resonator so that the sound remains the same right up the scale, but the pitch is changing with each note and is brought about by a tightening of the vocal cords and a gradual closing of the *glottis* (the gap between the cords).

It is possible to analyse each speech sound and thus to determine what frequencies it is comprised of, and how much of each frequency is required to produce the particular sound. Harvey

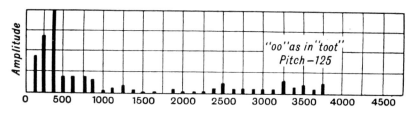

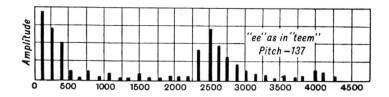

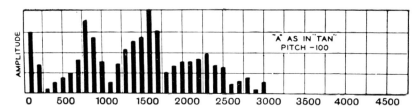

Figure 19. Each sound is comprised of different frequency components.

Fletcher, in his classic textbook of 1929, drew attention to this and analysed many of the phonemes. Figure 19 represents three vowels which have been analysed to show the amounts of each frequency which go to make up the sounds as we know them.

It is seen from these graphs then, that [u] as in "shoe" is comprised mainly of low frequency sound round about the 500 cycles level. However, [i] as in "sheep" has a band of pressure at the lower end of the scale, and then a second concentration of sound round about the 2,500 to 3,000 cycles level, and these two bands give the sound its particular quality.

THE PRODUCTION OF CONSONANTS

Consonants are caused when an obstruction occurs in the flow of the breath stream.

Classification

(a) Consonants are classified into two types according to whether they are *voiced* or *unvoiced*, e.g., "p" and "b," "s" and "z," "k" and "g," etc.

(b) They may be further classified by considering "where" the obstruction occurs to the breath stream, e.g., the consonant "P" occurs when the lips block the airstream and the sound is in consequence known as a "bilabial."

(c) A third method of classification is derived by noting "the nature" of the obstruction. In "k," for example, air pressure is built up at the back of the mouth, and then suddenly released with a little explosion—all such consonants, e.g., p, b, t, d, k, g are known as *plosives*. Others are caused by the friction of air passing through a narrow gap, e.g., f and v, [θ] and [ð], [ʃ] and [z] etc., and are known as *fricatives*.

Using the above three methods of classification we may thus describe consonants as follows: "b" is a voiced, bilabial, plosive consonant; "[θ]" is an unvoiced, palato-dental, fricative, etc.

It may be seen from Table 2 that the unvoiced consonants in running speech have no really low frequency components—all beginning at about 1500 cycles or higher, and that all consonants voiced and unvoiced, have important high frequencies which are critical to their intelligibility.

It should be remembered that there is a very important difference in the frequency spectrum of consonants which are said in normal running speech and those which are said in isolation and forced (as is often the case in speech teaching). There is a distinct lowering of the frequency components in fricatives when forced, and in plosives, many become like "White noise," i.e., a multi-frequency sound, all appearing to be very much the same—rather like the indefinite "breathy" sound which results when someone blows across a microphone in a hall to test the amplifying system.

Children who are very deaf may be enabled to hear the sound of consonants, but the majority can never hope to hear them intelligibly nor to discriminate between them. (It is of tremendous importance in speech teaching with such children, for the teacher to show by his or her facial expression when the child is saying the sound incorrectly, nearly correctly and finally correctly.)

THE SONA-GRAPH

Analysing the frequency components of speech is not an easy matter because the range of frequencies is so complex and each syllable is so fleeting. The invention of the *Sona-Graph* has provided a very satisfactory means of analysing a short sample of speech material. Other sounds can, of course, be analysed with it; bird songs, animal noises, the sound stimuli which are used in tests of hearing for very young children, etc.

TABLE 2

FREQUENCIES OF CONSONANTS

θ					About 6000
o	250–300				4500 – 6000
s					5000 – 6000
z	200 –300				4000 – 5000
f					4500 – 5000
v	300 – 400				3500 – 4500
t				2500 – 3500	
d	300 – 400			2500 – 3000	
k	300 – 400			2000 – 2500	
g	200 – 300			2000 – 3000	
l	250 – 400			2000 – 3000	
p			1500 – 2000		
b	300 – 400			2000 – 3000	
h			1500 – 2000		
sh			1500 – 2000		4500 – 5500
ch			1500 – 2000		4000 – 5000
j	200 – 300			2000 – 3000	
m	250 – 350	1000 – 1500		2500 – 3500	
n	250 – 350	1000 – 1500		2500–3000	
ng	250 – 400	1000 – 1500		2000 – 3000	
r	600 –800	1000–1500		2000 – 2400	

Adapted from Harvey Fletcher (1929): *Speech and Hearing.* van Nostrand. (Sounds analysed during quiet conversational speech.)

Figure 20. The Sona-Graph—An instrument for analysing sounds.

Figure 21. The Sonagram. Analysis of a short sample of running speech.

	Joe	took	father's	shoe - bench	out
c.p.s.	150	140	145	180	110	110

Variations in the pitch of vowel sounds in conversational speech.

The *Sona-Graph* (Fig. 20), analyses any sound signal as a function of both time and frequency. The resultant portrayal, known as a sonagram, displays frequency along the vertical axis, time along the horizontal axis and intensity by the darkness of the pattern (Fig. 21). Frequency is shown up to 8,000 cycles in a vertical distance of four inches (those included here have been reduced in size). The sonagram covers a period of time equivalent to 2.4 seconds for a horizontal distance of approximately 12.5 inches.

In operation, the wanted signal, e.g., a phrase, is first recorded on a magnetic disc. It is played back over and over again. On each repetition, the signal is scanned by either a 45 cycle or a 300 cycle band-pass filter, i.e., the first filter lets through a narrow band of frequencies—say from 500-545 cycles to begin with. At each repetition the filter is effectively shifted in frequency, e.g., from 500-545 to 505-550 and then from 510-555, etc.

The output of the analysing filter is then recorded on dry facsimile paper (Fig. 21) that is fastened around a rotating drum. The recording stylus shifts gradually up the frequency scale in step with the scanning oscillator.

Let us consider very briefly the sample of speech, "Joe took father's shoe bench out," as portrayed in Figure 21. This phrase is one which has been used in the Bell Telephone Laboratories for many years because it contains a variety of sounds which are strategically placed for analysing purposes.

The [dʒ] in "Joe" is seen here to be of short duration and mostly of frequencies above 2,000 cycles. [oʊ] is a clear diphthong which in this case was comprised of four *formants*—dark bands representing the frequencies where the sound was greatest. The [t] of "took" and of "out" are short and although as Fletcher suggests in Table 2, most of the energy is between 2,500 and 3,500, a certain amount of the plosive contains lower frequencies. This is possibly due to a slight degree of forcing as this sound was said. The [ʊ] sound in "took" is seen to be very short in duration, a fact not always appreciated by teachers of the deaf, and the k, f, b, and h, as said here, were scarcely audible—all these consonants acting rather as complete blocks to the air stream rather than displaying their distinctive frequencies as when said in isolation. [z] and [ʃ] are interesting—due to some forcing, both sounds are rather lower in frequency than one would expect (Table 2), but each is clearly defined and the [z] is seen to glide into the lower frequency [ʃ] sound. The second and third formants of [ɛ] in "bench" can be seen to be bending upwards as the mouth opens from the plosive [b].

It is possible by counting the number of the vertical striations in the phonemes to calculate the frequency of the fundamental or laryngeal tone of each. This was done for six of the seven vowels displayed in Figure 21.

It is interesting that the stressed syllable ("shoe") should be so much higher in pitch than the other sounds. Changes in pitch between vowels of up to 100 cycles are not uncommon.

Vowel formants are labelled F_1, F_2, F_3, etc. in the order in which they occur in the frequency scale. The fundamental voice frequency is labelled F_0. The first formant (F_1) is usually the strongest. There are always two formants and often a third, associated with each vowel (Fig. 23).

The relative importance of the formants of voiced sounds decreases above F_2. F_3 and F_4 contribute to certain vowel sounds and with F_0, account for speaker differences, but F_1 and F_2 govern the essential character of the sound.

The fact that some of the frequency components of vowel sounds analysed here vary quite considerably from Harvey Fletcher's published data, may be caused to some extent by the fact that he refers to American speakers whereas the accent recorded here is a New Zealand one.

INTENSITIES OF SPEECH SOUNDS

Not all speech sounds are of the same strength. The sounds [ɔ], [ʌ], [ou], [aɪ], and [au], for example, are about 20db. louder than p or b or d. In Table 3, the relative strengths of all the sounds are given when used in conversational speech and these are graphed in Figure 22.

The mean intensity of the twelve vowels and diphthongs measured above is 56.90 db. and that of the twenty consonants 43.97 db. There is no point in students or teachers learning Table 3 by heart: (a) because the list is incomplete; (b) because the

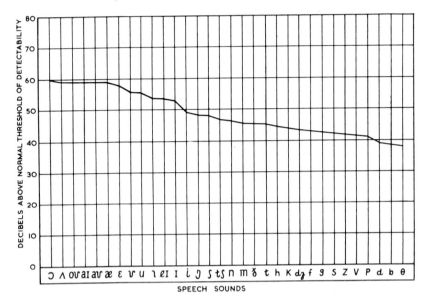

Figure 22. Relative intensities of sounds during normal conversational
speech.

differences in the intensity of so many of the sounds is so very
slight, and (c) because the order of ranking as given here is very
frequently upset by the use of *accent* and *emphasis*, and by speech

TABLE 3

ABOVE NORMAL THRESHOLD OF DETECTABILITY

Relative Intensity Levels of 32 Sounds Analysed
During Normal Conversational Speech.

ɔ	for	60 db	n		46.8
ʌ	cup	59.6	m		45.4
oʊ	home	59.6	ð	the	44.2
aɪ	mine	59.5	t		44.1
aʊ	cow	59.2	h		43.9
æ	cat	59.2	k		43.8
ε	ten	58.4	dʒ	jump	43.7
ʊ	took	55.9	f		43.6
u	school	55.9	g		42.9
l	let	53.5	s		42.4
eɪ	play	53.5	z		41.6
ɪ	bit	52.6	v		41.4
i	team	49.4	p		40.6
ŋ	ring	48.9	d		38.9
ʃ	shop	48.9	b		38.8
tʃ	chop	47.2	θ	thin	38.7

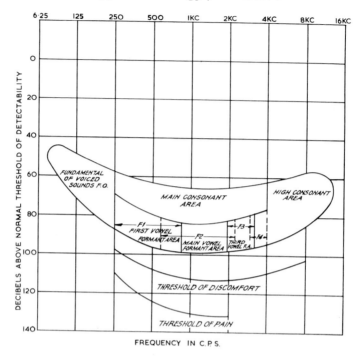

Figure 23. Formant areas of vowels and consonants. (Male data level above A.S.A. free field threshold at 2 cm. from lips of speaker, from Wedenberg.)

differences. Fletcher [62] states that "syllabic power varies more with the emphasis given than with the vowel used. A vowel in an accented syllable has three or four times as much phonetic power as one in an unaccented syllable." The Ewings [56] give as an example of this: "This is a very short corridor," saying that the intensity of the vowel in "short" would be three or four times greater than that in "corridor." They go on to agree with Fletcher that trained speakers probably stress the weaker sounds of speech rather more than do those who are untrained, and suggest that where such emphasis is given, the speech is better heard by patients with defective hearing.

In view of the above variables, if one remembers that very often consonants are roughly 10 or 15 db. weaker than vowels and diphthongs, it is as much as one needs to know with regards the intensities of phonemes.

Information about frequencies and intensities of speech sounds, which were analysed by Fant,[60, 61] has been summarised in graph form by Wedenberg (Fig. 23).[198] The latter's scheme of auditory training has been briefly referred to on page 107.

Chapter 5

SPEAKER DIFFERENCES AND ACOUSTIC CONDITIONS

SPEAKER DIFFERENCES

Beranek (1954)[8] has quoted Egan (1944),[42] who showed that different speakers were heard with varying degrees of intelligibility by adult listeners with normal auditory acuity. Four radio announcers read PB words in quiet and noisy conditions. In quiet, the most intelligible speaker obtained 95 per cent of correct word articulation and the least intelligible, 90 per cent. He found that differences in intelligibility between speakers were much more significant in noise; the most intelligible was 70 per cent and the least 45 per cent.

Palmer,[156] however, could find no difference in the intelligibility of nine trained speakers (three men, three women, and three twelve-year-old girls) when PB words were read to thirteen adult partially hearing listeners. Six of the group had hearing impairments which were perceptive in origin and the remainder suffered from conductive deafnesses. Palmer did not state whether the partially hearing group listened aided or unaided.

Nearly all hearing aid users comment upon the differences in intelligibility of the voices of various speakers. Some feel they hear male voices better than female ones, others that people who use a rapid or "staccato" type of delivery are difficult to hear through a hearing aid, and all seem to agree that there is a breathy or "catarrhal" type of voice which is particularly difficult to hear.

It has been possible to show that very significant differences do exist in the intelligibility of the speech of several speakers for children with perceptive (nerve) deafnesses who were wearing hearing aids. (Dale,[26] pp. 199-201) A group of ten speakers recorded one list each of the adapted M/J word list test.* The

---
* See Chapter 2, Speech Tests of Hearing.

speakers consisted of eight teachers of the deaf who had been selected at random (except that four were men and four were women), and one male and one female graduate. Twenty children were divided into two groups of ten,† and each listened to five speakers. The scores obtained by the two groups showed that differences existed in the intelligibility of the ten speakers.

In Group 1 the speaker who was most intelligible scored 68 per cent correct, whilst the least intelligible speaker scored only 43.5 per cent. In Group 2, the best and worst mean scores were 72.3 per cent and 48.0 per cent, respectively. Twenty "t" tests were made between mean scores obtained for each two speakers, and in eleven cases the differences were found to be significant at the one per cent level of confidence. In three other cases, differences were significant at the 5 per cent level.

If one teacher's voice is only two-thirds as intelligible as another (as is the case with the extremes quoted above), this would seem to be a sufficiently important factor to be given consideration in the selection and training of teachers of deaf children. Had a larger sample of teachers been taken, the discrepancies might well have been much greater.

The question arises as to whether less intelligible speech is remediable. It was noted, for example, that the two speakers who were heard least well had very poor breath control. Neither was in the habit of breathing deeply and one stated that she had "never been able to shout properly." Both voices lacked resonance and this showed up very clearly when sonagrams were made of them.

Figure 24 represents recordings of the speakers who were heard best in each group and those who were heard least well. Comparisons of these reveal significant differences in the formant spectra of the vowels. Sonagram A is that of the male speaker whose speech was most intelligible. Vowels and consonants are nearly all clearly defined. The third and fourth vowel formants are clear, and the vertical striations show the voice to be deep in pitch and well modulated. $[o\upsilon] = 150$ c/s, $[u] = 180$ c/s and $[\varepsilon] = 100$ c/s. Sonagram B is that of the female speaker who was most intelligible. Prior to her training as a teacher of the deaf,

† The mean hearing loss of Group 1 was 63.25 db. and of Group 2, 67.42 db.

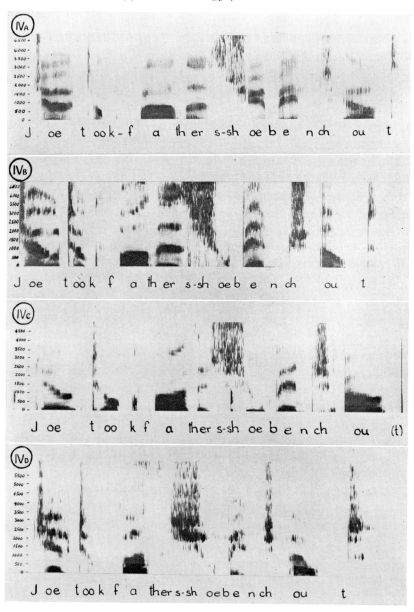

Figure 24. Analyses of the frequency components of the voices of four speakers. (A and B were heard well, C and D were heard poorly.)

this person had been a BBC announcer. Again all the vowel formants except the [u] of "shoe bench" are strongly portrayed and the consonants are very well defined. There is perhaps a little more *fill* between the formants than is the case in A. The laryngeal tone or pitch of the voice was rather low in frequency and the voice well modulated [oʊ] = 220 c/s, [u] = 290 c/s and [ɛ] = 190 c/s. Sonagrams C and D, however, portray extremely poor vowel formants in nearly every instance. Those which are particularly defective are the neutral vowel [ə] in "father," and the long [u] of "shoe bench." None of the vowels or diphthongs is rich in harmonics with the exception of [oʊ] in "Joe" in D and here the formants lack definition. The consonants are fairly clear, though not possessing the precision of those of the male speaker.

Further research is required to ascertain more clearly the reason for the intelligibility and the causes of the unintelligibility of various voices. Investigations to find out to what extent unintelligible voices are remediable are also indicated.

ACOUSTIC CONDITIONS

Acoustics. Not a great deal has been written about the importance of acoustic conditions to hearing aid users, yet it is fairly easy to illustrate that the type of listening conditions which prevail in a room can be critical to the successful use of a hearing aid. Not nearly enough attention has in the past been paid to the acoustics of classrooms for normally hearing children, let alone those for deaf and partially hearing ones. J. E. J. John and H. Thomas [115] have made very practical suggestions for the siting and construction of buildings which are to be used by children wearing aids. Two aspects of acoustic conditions concern the hearing aid user, noise and reverberation.

Noise

Harold [86] showed: (a) that hearing for speech was adversely affected by noise, but that it did not alter the level of intensity at which optimum hearing took place. This may explain why so many hearing aid users rarely adjust their hearing aid volume controls in varying acoustic conditions.

(b) That nerve deafened cases heard speech much less well

in noise than did subjects with conductive deafnesses. It is thus of considerable importance to reduce noise levels in schools and classes for deaf children, since all but a handful of such children suffer from deafness which is perceptive in origin.

As John and Thomas emphasise, it is best to eliminate noise at its source rather than try to exclude it once it is produced.

External noise, from traffic or from industry, can create impossible listening conditions—noise levels up to 100-120 db. Careful siting of school buildings is therefore most essential.

"If the use of a site with a noise level of greater than 70 db. is unavoidable, extensive and expensive insulation is necessary."

Trees, evergreen hedges, artificial embankments, and the erection of other buildings between the source of the noise and the classrooms, all improve listening conditions. Double glazing is another very effective means of excluding noise from rooms, but it is then usually necessary to install ventilators which are often costly.

There is not a great deal that class teachers can do about controlling external noise—except, of course, to keep on complaining if it is really bad.

Internal noise, from corridor and stair traffic, from toilets, and from adjoining classrooms. Four inch brick walls, discontinuous flooring, and floor coverings of rubber or some such resilient material have all been helpful in reducing noises created within the building but outside the classroom.

Room noise from moving of furniture, shuffling of feet, turning pages, opening and closing drawers, artificial ventilation systems, etc. Children can be trained to be reasonably quiet in their movements about a room and when shifting tables or chairs. The use of rubber pads on chair and table legs is well worthwhile. Sheet rubber over foam rubber is probably the best type of floor covering, but other substitutes are available which seem almost as effective and durable and which are much less expensive. A well-covered floor is a tremendous help in reducing room noise.

Knudsen and Harris [122] recommended that for ordinary children, classroom noise should not exceed 35-40 db. above .0002 dynes/cm^2. The Ministry of Education [141] suggested that 25-30 phons was permissible in classrooms for ordinary children.

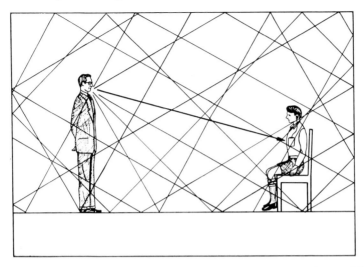

Figure 25. Behaviour of sound in a reverberant room. (Much simplified.) (N.B. Interference with teacher's speech before it reaches the child's microphone.)

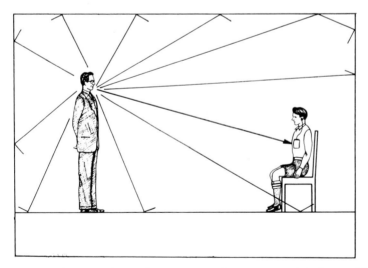

Figure 26. Behaviour of sound in a nonreverberant room. (Much simplified.)

John [115] regarded 25-30 phons as the minimum requirement in schools for the deaf.

Reverberation

The term *reverberation* is roughly synonymous with *echo*. When a person speaks in a room, the sound of the voice travels out (in compressions and rarefactions), at a speed of 1,100 feet per second. On striking an object such as a wall or floor or ceiling, the sound is deflected and carries on to the next obstruction, where it is deflected again, and so on. If the surface of the obstruction met is hard and shiny, the sound rebounds with little loss of energy (Fig. 25). Tiled bathrooms, for example, are very reverberant places.

If the surface is soft or has been covered with good quality sound absorbent lagging material, then the sound enters the material (acoustic tiles, carpets, soft furnishings, etc.) and much of its energy is dissipated by generating heat or by causing movements of the surfaces. In Figure 26, the sound is seen to be "killed" at the walls, floor and ceiling, and in consequence there is much less distortion of the sounds created in the room.

The diagrams are very much simplified just to emphasise the effect of acoustic treatment. In fact, even in a well treated classroom, a sound of 60 db. would bounce from wall to wall twenty or thirty times before it became inaudible.

John [113] reported the results of experiments which showed the effect of speaking at varying distances from a microphone, on the speech reception scores of normal listeners. Word lists were recorded on magnetic tape at distances of three inches, six inches, eighteen inches, three feet and nine feet. When delivered through a group hearing aid at a level of 65 db. above detectability, the articulation scores obtained were 96 per cent, 94 per cent, 80 per cent, 72 per cent, and 65 per cent respectively. The reverberation time existing in the room in which the tests were made approximated that of the "traditional type of classroom," and John concluded that reverberation could seriously limit the value of hearing aids for children. He maintained that due to wide differences from room to room it was difficult to lay down acoustic standards which could be universally applied. He suggested, however, that for small classrooms, as were commonly found in schools for the deaf, satisfactory results could be obtained if a quarter of the surface was treated with good quality absorbent materials. Usually, if the ceiling and about the top three to four feet of the walls are covered, the treatment is quite effective.

It was thought advisable to compare the scores obtained by children wearing hearing aids in the poor acoustic conditions existing in some classrooms with those obtained when they were tested in the good acoustic conditions of an audiology clinic. The group consisted of twelve children aged between ten and fifteen years whose mean I.Q. was 106·00 (S.D. 20·6). All were attending ordinary schools. The tests were made at varying distances from the microphone. The opportunity was also taken to ascertain how suitable listening conditions were in these classrooms for children with normal hearing.

In the classrooms, before each test began, the partially hearing child was asked to sit in the front row directly in front of the speaker. All the class were given sheets of paper on which three columns of numbers had been cyclostyled. The following instructions were given: "I am going to say some words and I want you to write down what I say. They are quite simple words like "house," "boat," "dog," and so on. If you don't hear a word clearly, write what you think it was or put a dash. Don't worry if you don't hear a word properly, and don't try to find out what it was from anyone sitting near you. Do you understand what to do?" An M/J word list was then delivered which was monitored at 70 db., eighteen inches from the speaker. Each word was preceded by the carrier phrase, "Number . . . is." This served the dual purpose of building up reverberation in the room and ensuring that the children did not lose the place in the list. At the completion of the first list the partially deaf child was moved to a position about half way down the classroom (at twelve to sixteen feet from the speaker), and the next list was given. The partially hearing child then sat on the back row (twenty to twenty-four feet from the speaker), and the last list was read. The children who had been sitting at four to eight feet from the speaker were then asked to write "A" on their papers, those at twelve to sixteen feet "B," and at twenty to twenty-four feet "C."

Similar tests were made again with the partially hearing children in a clinic which had been well treated acoustically. On this

TABLE 4

ARTICULATION SCORES OBTAINED IN DIFFERENT ACOUSTIC
CONDITIONS BY TWELVE PARTIALLY HEARING CHILDREN

Distance from microphone	12″	4′	14′	22′
Good listening conditions	84%	70.8%		64 %
Poor listening conditions		54.4%	44.8%	39.2%

occasion the M/J lists were delivered at twelve inches, four feet and twenty-two feet from the microphone.

Table 4 illustrates the detrimental effect on intelligibility which results from varying the distance of the speaker from the microphone in very reverberant and slightly reverberant conditions.

The table emphasises the finding of John [113] (with normally hearing subjects) that the drop in intelligibility is most marked in the first few feet as one moves away from the microphone, e.g., in the good conditions there was a drop in intelligibility of about 13 per cent in the first three feet, but of only 7 per cent in the next eighteen feet. The importance of speaking close to the microphone is clearly illustrated. It will be shown later that this is not always practical to arrange in the classroom situation, but teachers and others should realise the value of speaking close to the microphone wherever it is possible to do so.

The decrease in intelligibility is much more rapid in poor acoustic conditions than is the case in quiet and non-reverberant ones.

It is possible to illustrate the effect on speech induced by varying distances from a microphone in good and in poor acoustic conditions by means of sonagrams (Figs. 27 and 28). The sentence, "Joe took father's shoe bench out," has been recorded direct on to the Sona-Graph recorder at twelve inches, six feet, and fifteen feet from the microphone in good and in poor acoustic conditions. The recordings in the nonreverberant conditions were made in the clinic in which the children had been tested (reverberation time <1 second). The input to the microphone was maintained at 70 db. for all recordings by monitoring with a

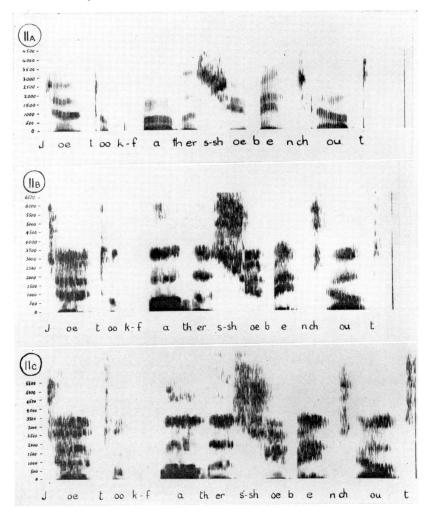

Figure 27. Effect of speaking at various distances from the microphone in good acoustic conditions.

sound level meter. The wide band filter was used when the sonagram was run off.

Figure 27, Sonagram A (twelve inches in good acoustic conditions) shows a distinct record with frequency formants for the vowels clearly defined.

In Figure 27, Sonagram B (six feet in good acoustic condi-

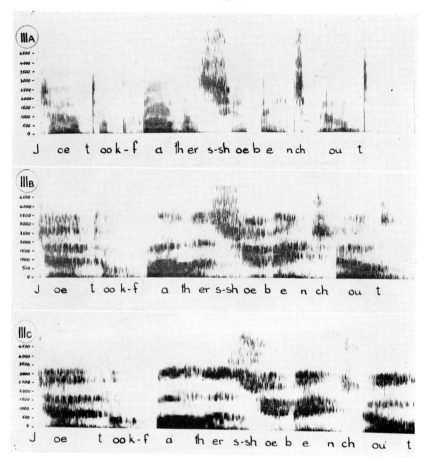

Figure 28. Speaking at various distances from the microphone in poor acoustic conditions.

tions), both vowels and consonants have lost a considerable degree of definition (see particularly [u] in "shoe bench"), and the formants appear somewhat "smudgy." Due to the reverberation, the vowels have lengthened slightly and are beginning to "overrun" or mask the consonants (c.f., [a] in "father's").

When speaking fifteen feet from the microphone a further deterioration in the clarity of all sounds is perceptible, with formants tending to merge one into another (c.f., second and third formants of [ɛ] in "bench"). The gap which represented [ð] in "father" is seen to have closed considerably, but those for the sounds [k, f, b, and n] are still present although somewhat reduced.

Under reverberant acoustic conditions, distance from the microphone can be seen to be of critical importance to intelligible speech reception (Fig. 28). At twelve inches from the microphone (Fig. 28, Sonagram A), the pattern is relatively clear, although not as distinct as in the non-reverberant room at the same distance. At six feet and fifteen feet, however, reverberation is seen to produce marked perseverations in the vowel formants which mutilate the form of the consonants. When the sonagrams of Figures 27 and 28 are studied, it is not surprising that articulation scores obtained under these conditions differ by almost 50 per cent.

Chapter 6

BEST LISTENING LEVELS

Just how loud speech must be made to give each deaf person the best possible listening experience has concerned a large number of workers in audiology. Despite this, by no means the last word has been said on this interesting subject. Before considering the present position it is necessary, however, to consider very briefly the method by which optimum levels are obtained.

THE ARTICULATION FUNCTION

(a) The Articulation Score. When a list of words is read to a subject, the number of words he hears correctly is known as his *articulation score.* Thus, if he hears twenty-five words correctly out of fifty, he has an articulation score of twenty-five (or of fifty per cent).

(b) The Articulation Curve. Word lists may be presented quietly or loudly. When they are delivered at various levels of loudness to a subject, it is possible to plot a graph of the scores obtained (Fig. 29). This graph is called an *articulation curve.* Modern audiometry, according to Carhart [18] is based on the concept of the articulation function, i.e., the relationship between the percentage of speech items heard correctly by the subject and the intensity at which the items were delivered.

(The word *articulation* is derived from testing the fidelity of telephone communication systems—workers need to know how closely the speech sounds received by the listener "articulated" with those presented by the speaker in the other room, or building or city. Articulation score as used in the remainder of this section has nothing at all to do with a person's ability to say sounds correctly.)

As can be seen in Figure 29, articulation curves may vary a great deal in shape from one subject to another. Factors which

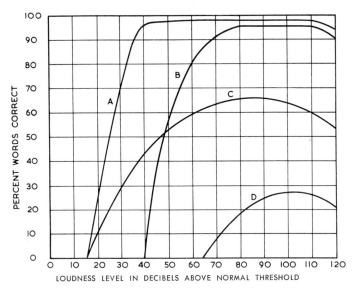

Figure 29. Articulation curves for four subjects.

affect the shape of the curve have been considered by various writers to include: the deafness of the subject; [171] the type of speech material used; [97] the intelligence, education and interests of the subject; [157] the type of amplifying equipment used, the voice of the speaker (Fletcher [62] p. 255); and the aetiology of the deafness.[38, 171, 127] Walsh and Silverman,[187] and Davis [28] and many others have shown that for pure conductive deafnesses, the shape of the curve remains the same as for normally hearing subjects (Fig. 29–Curve A), but is displaced to the right, that is to say, the most difficult words are heard correctly if they are presented loudly enough (Fig. 29–Curve B).

For subjects with severe perceptive deafness, however, most writers agree that no matter what level of amplification is used, 100 per cent intelligibility is seldom attained [121, 28, 157, 127] (Fig. 29–Curves C and D).

OPTIMUM LISTENING LEVELS

When subjects have normal hearing, the articulation curve has been found to flatten at an average of 35 db. above detectability, i.e., subjects attain maximum intelligibility at that level (Egan [43]). From the following literature, it may be seen that this factor tended to dominate the thinking of workers in ascertaining best listening levels.

Liden suggested that if the articulation curves for patients with various types of hearing losses did not diverge unduly from the normal, it should be possible to determine optimum levels for setting amplifying apparatus by simply adding 35 db. to their thresholds of detectability. In practice he found that in many cases such predictions could be inaccurate. Liden also drew attention to the fact that where the hearing loss was pronounced, the level of uncomfortable loudness became a limiting factor to any such fixed increment of amplification, e.g., if a person's hearing loss was 100 db., 135 db. of output might well be much too loud for him. In his study of 104 patients, sixty of whom had auditory impairments which were conductive in origin, Liden [127] gave consideration to the relationship between the level at which maximum score on word lists occurred and the level of most comfortable loudness of the subjects. In many cases, the latter were found to be only 20 db. above the patients' thresholds of detectability. He concluded that comfort levels were not necessarily a valid criterion for obtaining optimum amplification levels.

Bangs [4] suggested that one reason for obtaining accurate pure tone thresholds for young deaf children was to determine how much amplification should be given each child. She then outlined the procedure she adopted for setting listening levels; the output at the receiver should first be set approximately 15 db. above the child's average pure tone loss. After a four- to six-week training period, Bangs noted an increased tolerance for loud sound. During this time, she recommended a gradual increase in amplification from 15 to 30 db. "if feasible."

Pickles [160] worked with eighty-nine pre-school children attending an audiology clinic. She claimed that for children whose thresholds of detectability were less than 80 db., listening experience was best begun at 90 db. above the normal threshold of detectability, and increased "step by step to reach 30 db. above threshold and further if it was found beneficial." For the children whose thresholds of detectability for voice lay between 80 and

95 db., first listening experience was given at 10 db. above their threshold of detectability and they were then "encouraged to listen at the highest intensities" (*Ibid.*, p. 83).

In the Department of Education of the Deaf at Manchester University, for many years, the procedure for obtaining the correct listening level with children unable to co-operate in speech tests was: (a) to find the child's threshold of detectability for voice, and (b) to add 30 db. to this (if it were practical to do so).

While investigating volume control adjustment in connection with hearing aid selection, Carhart [51] made a study of the reliability of the comfort level method of setting hearing aid volume controls. Using 413 partially deaf subjects, he found that the test-retest reliability of this method was high (r = .87).

Harold's Suggested Listening Levels

Harold [86] conducted the most comprehensive investigation so far into the best listening levels for children with hearing defects up to 90 db. He showed quite conclusively that the practice of adding a fixed increment, such as 30 or 35 db., to a threshold of detectability, or to a pure tone hearing loss was a most unsound means of obtaining a best listening level. After constructing articulation curves for 182 children, an attempt was made to devise a method by which suitable volume settings could be predicted from audiograms. Consideration was given to three intensity levels in the proximity of the best one and the following levels were found to represent the point of maximum score or within 90 per cent of maximum score, for 80 per cent of the cases:

TABLE 5

Hearing Loss	Optimum Listening Level
Between 30–50	80 db. above the normal threshold of detectability
Between 50–75	90 db. above the normal threshold of detectability
Between 75–90	100 db. above the normal threshold of detectability
Greater than 90	The loudest level that could be comfortably tolerated

Harold was careful to point out that a formula which was only accurate four times out of five could not be recommended for general application. He suggested, however, that it might prove useful in situations where it was not possible to apply other methods to ascertain optimum listening levels.

Because his sample contained few children whose hearing losses exceeded 90 db., Harold was unable to make any firm statement about best levels for this group. He did say, however, that "It would seem that for the most part, these cases responded best to speech at the loudest level they could comfortably tolerate." Another important factor which Harold's investigation emphasised was that the intensity range over which perceptively deafened children heard best was in most cases a very limited one. Of the 155 children in the group whose losses were perceptive in origin: 43 per cent obtained their maximum score at one level only; 25 per cent obtained their best score or within 10 per cent of maximum at two levels 10 db. apart; and the remaining 32 per cent attained maximum score or within 10 per cent of maximum at three levels, i.e., over a range of 20 db. (percentages quoted are approximate).

From the foregoing discussion of listening levels, it may be assumed that all four writers considered the optimum setting for children whose hearing impairments exceeded 90 db., to be the maximum intensity which they could comfortably tolerate.

Silverman [174] reported that thresholds of discomfort, tickle and pain rose systematically and significantly with successive test sessions. Huizing also suggested that tolerance levels could be raised by approximately 10 db. over a period of weeks. Harold drew attention to the difficulty of obtaining an "unvarying criterion for discomfort, particularly with naïve listeners." He considered that many of the low discomfort levels recorded in his research may have been a reflection of the psychological approach to the stimulus rather than the result of "pathological disturbances." Evidence to support this contention is easy to obtain, particularly with the profoundly and sub-totally deaf children. When setting the listening level for these children using a speech training aid, the intensity is often carefully increased, in 5 db. steps. Very frequently the children will grimace or say "too loud" within 5 db. of their threshold of detectability, but if, after a few minutes of talking to the child at this level, the output is unobtrusively increased, they frequently accept the higher level without complaint. When, for example, this technique was used in a study of twenty children with impairments in excess of 100 db.,[26] all but four were tested at a level of 135 db. above .0002 dynes/cm^2 and of these four, two preferred 130 db. and two, 125.

Whilst agreeing with the statement by Silverman and Huizing that the initial level of discomfort is lower than that achieved later, it has been my experience with very deaf children that levels of amplification can often be raised in a matter of minutes rather than weeks. Many such children are naïve to sound—in not a few cases they are found not wearing hearing aids "because they are too deaf," or the aids with which they have been issued are not sufficiently powerful to reach them. For the children whose losses were less severe, Liden, Bangs and Pickles suggested an increase above their thresholds of detectability of a set amount—the former 35 db. (except for recruiting cases), and the two last named, 30 db. Harold, however, found that there were wide individual differences in the amount of amplification above detectability required. For example, a child whose hearing impairment was 35 db. might require 45 db. of amplification, while one whose loss was 90 db. might only require 10 db. above his threshold of detectability to obtain maximum intelligibility.

Harold's work suggests that the only reliable method to obtain the optimum level of amplification is to test each child individually. In those cases where speech tests prove impracticable, e.g., due to immaturity of the subject and/or an extremely limited vocabulary, the scale suggested by him, provided its limitations are recognised, seems most likely to obtain the best volume setting.

Just how accurately do deaf children set the volume controls of their hearing aids when they are asked to switch them on? An experiment was conducted with thirty-one partially and severely deaf children to help ascertain this. The age range of the group was between ten and fifteen years and the mean hearing loss 66.11 db., S.D. 13.5 db. An articulation curve was made for each child to find his best listening level. He was then asked to tell the investigator (who used a bracketing technique) when the hearing aid was set at the best listening level. (The speech circuit of an audiometer was used for both the articulation curves and the subjective adjustments of the volume control.)

It was found that the majority of these children set the volume control very near to their best listening level (Fig. 30). This agrees with Carhart's finding with 413 adults mentioned earlier. In ten cases, the level was chosen which coincided exactly with the optimum listening level as determined by the articulation tests. A further twelve choices were within 5 db. of the optimum and six were within 10 db. Two of the three remaining children chose 15 db. below their best level, and one preferred a level 20 db. above that at which he had obtained maximum articulation score.

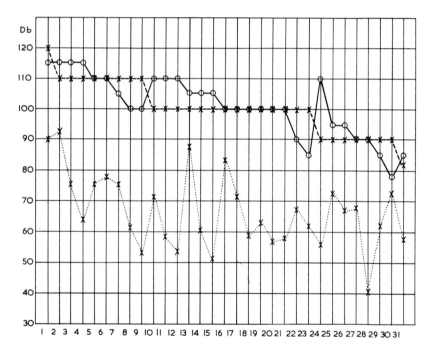

X--- = MAX. WORD LIST

O—— = CHILDREN'S SETTINGS

X······ = H. LOSS BETTER EAR

Figure 30. Comparison of subjective volume setting and best listening levels.

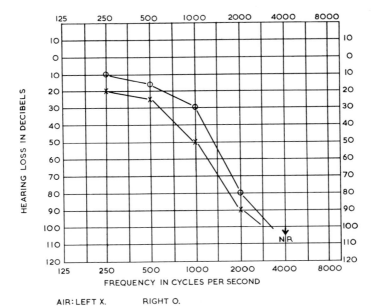

Figure 31A. Child No. 23.

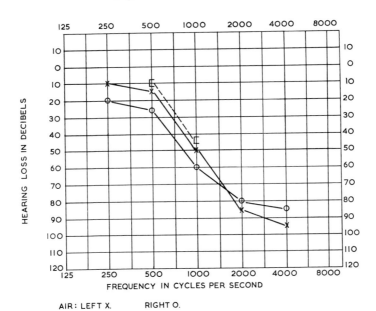

Figure 31B. Child No. 30.

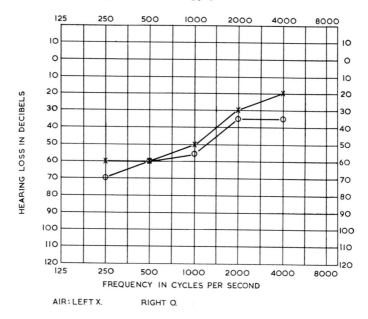

Figure 31C. Child No. 24.

The difference between these two sets of levels was not statistically significant (t = .38).

The audiograms of the three children who set the amplification most inaccurately were consulted. The two children who chose the level 15 db. below the best listening level (Nos. 23 and 30) had slight impairments at 250 cycles which deteriorated rapidly in the higher frequencies (Fig. 31, audiograms A and B).

Child No. 24, on the other hand, who set the control 20 db. above the lowest level at which he obtained maximum score, was seen to have the relatively rare shape of audiogram, with a fairly severe impairment over the lower frequency range and a rise (of 40 db. in one octave) for sounds at 2,000 c.p.s. which was maintained at 4,000 cycles (Fig. 31, audiogram C).

All three children were rated by their teachers as being of average intelligence. Further investigation of children who possess audiograms which slope steeply from the low to the higher frequencies, tends to confirm the findings of the first two cases cited above. A probable explanation is that the near normal hearing for low sounds makes them unpleasantly loud when amplified, and as a consequence such children quite understandably sacrifice a little intelligibility for a little comfort.

It seems possible that children with hearing losses which are less severe for the higher frequencies (like that shown in the right ear of Child No. 24) should not be troubled by increased amplification since sounds above 2,000 c.p.s. are not the strongest in speech and in consequence their amplification should not cause discomfort. Too few cases of this type have been examined, however, to draw any definite conclusions about them.

In the senior class of a nursery school for the deaf in London, however, where the children were seven years of age with hearing losses between 60 and 70 db. and had had several years experience of hearing aids, the majority appeared to have developed a considerable degree of skill in setting amplification levels. They would babble into the microphone of the group hearing aid or their individual aid and at the same time adjust the volume control. They would also report faults in their hearing aids very promptly.

YOUNG DEAF CHILDREN

No firm statement may be made regarding the ability of young deaf children to set hearing aids at their best listening levels, but teachers in nursery schools have found that the children in the beginners' class will accept a wide range of amplification without commenting that the level is too high or too low. In a day and residential nursery school, a 4½- to 5½-year-old class (with hearing losses between 75 and 87 db.) did state quite definitely if they could not hear or if the sound was uncomfortably loud, but again differences in settings of up to 35 db. were acceptable.

It appears that intelligence and the extent of the auditory impairment together with the length of previous auditory experience of the subject, are significant factors in determining the age at which skill in volume adjustment develops.

What can be done then with regards setting volume controls for these young deaf children? It will be clear that the table drawn up by Harold (Table 5), despite its limitations, represents the best guide to settings which is available at the present time.

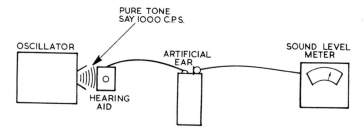

Figure 32. A diagrammatical representation of a hearing aid being tested on an artificial ear.

When one comes to apply this extremely useful information to the wearer of an individual hearing aid, however, one is immediately in difficulties. The volume controls of wearable hearing aids are seldom marked in decibels, and it is therefore not easy to ascertain what the output of the aid is at any setting. One solution is to have every hearing aid placed on an artificial ear (Fig. 32), but at present very few schools have access to these. *It is recommended here that if possible every hearing aid issued to a child or to an audiology unit should have with it technical data about the response curve of the instrument and the output which it gives at each position on the volume control.*

Where such information is not available, however, teachers and clinical workers must fall back on cruder but nevertheless useful subjective tests.

A teacher can, for example, ask an intelligent older child with an identical audiogram, to set the output of the preschool child's aid. When no audiogram is available for the preschooler, it is possible:

1. To use a speech training aid or an audiometer as a monitoring device, to give oneself an idea of a certain level, e.g., 100 db. above .0002 dynes per cm^2.
2. Without looking at the volume control switch the hearing aid to what seems to be the same level on it.
3. To note the point and repeat steps 1 and 2 several times.
4. To find other levels on the hearing aid control switch in the same manner.

One soon learns that although a hearing aid volume control may be marked from, say, 1 to 5, the output does not always increase in graded steps throughout this range.* Sometimes, for example, an aid gives no amplification at all at positions 1 and 2, then a sudden increase to position 3 which is maintained at this level through setting 4 and perhaps has a further increase in output at position 5. Teachers and parents should be aware of any peculiarities which exist in the children's hearing aid outputs. They should never be afraid to "have a listen" to any child's hearing aid or piece of amplifying apparatus. Suggestions are made in Chapter 8 for supervising and maintaining hearing aids.

In summary, there are four points which should be borne in mind with regards listening levels if the most intelligent use is to be made of hearing aids:

1. *The listening level should be set as accurately as possible.* It will be remembered that nearly half of the cases studied by Harold heard best at one point only—10 db. above or below this level caused a significant dropping off in the scores obtained.

2. *Older partially and severely deaf children seem in most cases to set the volume of their hearing aids with extreme accuracy.* The implication of this is not that checking listening levels with older children is unnecessary, but that such a check need not be made daily or even weekly after the initial best level has been determined.

3. *It is possible to increase levels of comfort with profoundly and sub-totally deaf subjects—particularly if they are naïve listeners.* It is suggested here, that one should not accept the first level indicated by these very deaf children, but should experiment after a few minutes with levels 5 or even 10 db. above the first level. This ensures that such subjects are then listening at "the loudest level they can comfortably tolerate."

4. *Younger deaf children frequently have very little idea of best listening levels.* The setting of volume controls is in consequence a very important part of the work of teachers, parents and others who deal with young deaf children.

---

* The Australian Government individual aid now has the output controlled in 5 db. steps.

Chapter 7

LOUDNESS RECRUITMENT

ONE OF THE BEST DEFINITIONS of loudness recruitment, is that of Hirsh, Palva and Goodman [91] who describe it as "a more than normal increase in subjective loudness for a given increase in physical intensity." To put it another way, a patient with recruitment, in spite of an impairment at threshold, hears loud sounds with a sensation of loudness equal or nearly equal to the loudness with which a normal ear would perceive them. There have been a large number of theories of what causes recruitment, but none seems yet to have been generally accepted. The hearing theory of Lorente de No (quoted by Nilsson [153]) is often used to give a theoretical explanation of recruitment occurring in all forms of nerve deafness. The theory is applied in this way. Where there has been damage to some of the neurones, there is a loss of sensitivity to sounds of low intensity, but where the intensity of the sound is high, other neurones will come into play to fill the demand, and the cortex will receive a sound equal in loudness to that of a normal ear. Since a slightly different pathway is used, the sound received may be qualitatively different from the original signal. Some recruiting patients, for example, reporting a change in the pitch of the sound, etc.

Lurie [135] explained loudness recruitment in terms of the differential functions of the inner and outer hair cells of the *organ of Corti* (Fig. 33A). He believed that the outer cells responded to the sounds of low intensity only, and that the inner cells responded to intensities of 30 db. and above. In the case of damage to the outer cells, the inner ones functioned normally, which accounts for the sensation of equal loudness. Tumarkin,[180, 181] De Bruine Altes,[35] Dix, Hallpike and Hood [37] were among those who gave favourable consideration to hair cell theories. The last named authors claiming that their evidence concerning the ab-

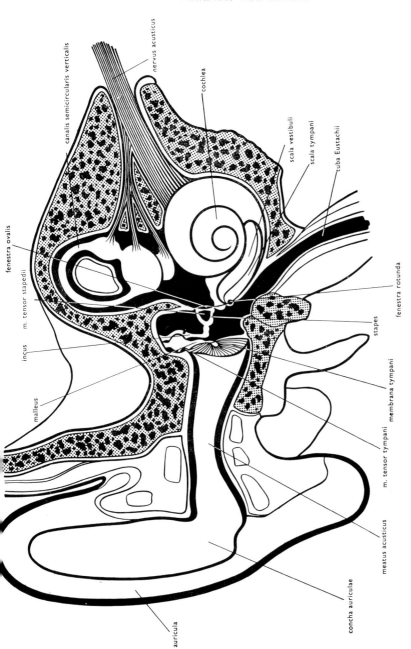

Figure 33A. Diagram of the outer, middle and inner ear.

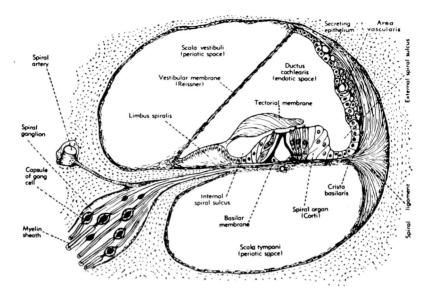

Figure 33B. Cross-section of the cochlea. (From A. T. Rasmussen (1943): *Outlines of Neuro-Anatomy*, 3rd Ed. Dubuque, Ia., Wm. C. Brown Co. Reproduced by permission of the publishers.)

sence of recruitment in cases of deafness caused by tumours of the eighth nerve (mentioned later) precludes the acceptance of the explanation given by Lorente de No. Recruitment, they contend, is always a symptom of a disorder of the hair cells.

Harold,[86] too, has produced evidence to suggest that recruitment was a result of malfunction of some part of the end organ of hearing, and could not find its presence in cases of eighth nerve disorders or cortical lesions.

It is an interesting phenomenon, which can be of considerable significance to audiologists and otologists for diagnostic purposes. For teachers of the deaf, however, recruitment is of very little importance, and if they are conversant with the following three facts about it, it is really all that it is necessary to know. (a) Full or partial recruitment seems to be present in about two-thirds of the children in schools and classes for the deaf and partially hearing, (b) if anything, children with recruitment tend to hear "better" than those without it, and (c) thresholds of discomfort are not lowered due to the presence of recruitment. It is commonly believed that children who do not seem able to tolerate loud sounds are suffering from recruitment, but this has not proved to be so.

The information contained in this section has been obtained very largely from the unpublished work of Dr. B. B. Harold,[86] with his kind permission.

Fowler,[65] as early as 1928, was the first to draw attention to the recruitment phenomenon. He observed that some patients with normal hearing in one ear and a considerable loss in the other sometimes heard a sound equally well in either ear. He devised a means of measuring this effect by allowing the patient to listen alternately with either ear while he increased the intensity. At a certain level, the sounds were heard equally loudly in both ears if recruitment was present (Fig. 34). His technique is known as the alternate binaural loudness balance test, and several loudness balance tests have been developed from it. Scott N. Reger,[165] for example, showed that recruitment could be demonstrated using one ear only as long as at least two frequencies had a large difference in threshold values. De Bruine Altes[33]

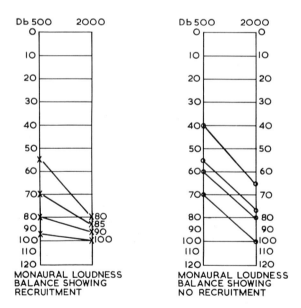

Figure 34. Method of recording loudness balance test results.

after a careful study suggested that it was not easy for an untrained ear to judge whether the loudness of two tones of different frequency were equal, but was of the opinion that the nearer in frequency the tones being compared, the more accurate was the test result likely to be.

The method of recording the loudness balance test results as adopted by Fowler [68] helps to make clear the effect of the recruitment phenomenon (Fig. 34). Two vertical lines are printed on the record sheet, each scaled in 10 db. steps from zero to 120. On the second line are marked the values of the reference tones used in the test and on the first are recorded the intensities of the test tones for which judgments of equal loudness have been made. Lines then join each equal loudness judgment with its appropriate reference tone.

Numerous tests for recruitment have been devised in addition to those involving loudness balance techniques. A type which has been given favourable consideration by a large number of work-

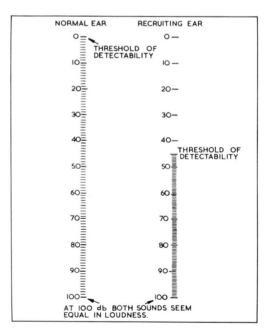

Figure 35.   Diagrammatical representation of the greater sensitivity of a recruiting ear to increments in loudness.

ers, however, is that which involves the *difference limen* for intensity. *The difference limen is the minimum increment in stimulus needed to produce a noticeable difference in sensation.*

According to Bangs and Mullins,[3] the rationale behind all types of test using the limen as a method of measuring loudness recruitment, is that the number of loudness units (difference limena) from the detectability of a sound to a sensation of equal loudness is approximately the same for both a normal and a recruiting ear, and since the threshold of the recruiting ear is elevated, the size of the difference limen must be smaller (Fig. 35). The argument is supported by experimental evidence as for example in the work of von Bekesy [7] and Luscher and Zwislocki.[136] They have found that recruiting patients *are* more sensitive to slight changes in sound intensity. Where normal and nonrecruiting ears are only able to detect changes of about 1 db. or more, a person with recruitment can detect changes of as little as .3 db., and occasionally even less than this.

Von Bekesy designed a special audiometer for his test. With it the subject records his own audiogram by noting the point at which a tone becomes audible and the point where it becomes just inaudible. The tone presented constantly changes in frequency. The recorded graph (Fig. 36) of the subject's responses claims to give the relative size of the difference limen at threshold.

Luscher and Zwislocki, on the other hand, give their test at 40 db. above threshold (or at 15-20 dbs. above in the case of very deaf subjects). In this test, a pure tone which varies in intensity is presented to the subject. If this variation is great—say 3 db.— we all hear it as a beating tone. As the amount of intensity change is reduced, the sound to normal ears gradually loses its sensation of *beat* and is heard as a tone of constant intensity. As has been stated, however, recruiting subjects with their small difference limena, can detect much smaller variations in intensity than can those without recruitment.

Denes and Naunton [34] devised a somewhat similar test, and Jerger [105, 106] combined some of the features of both tests to evolve a new method using an ascending method of presentation, i.e., the subject listens first to a constant tone and the amplitude modulation is increased until it is observed as a beat. Like Denes

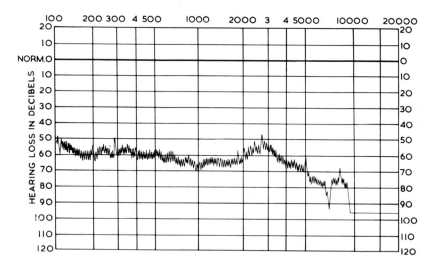

Figure 36A.

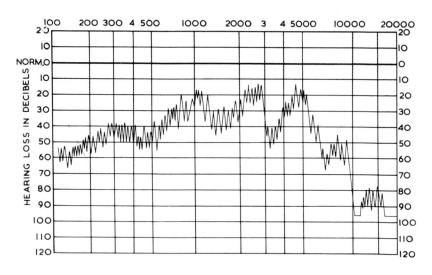

Figure 36B.

Figure 36. Bekesy audiograms: A. Of an ear with recruitment. B. Of a
nonrecruiting ear.

and Naunton, Jerger tested at two levels but they were 10 and 40 dbs. rather than 4 and 44 dbs. above threshold.

Although there are available, a wide variety of tests, the detection of recruitment is very often difficult and uncertain. In consequence, therefore, many workers have listed symptoms of the phenomenon which can be used in the clinical situations as a supplement to the more formal tests. Unfortunately, there is not always agreement on such symptoms being a true indication of the presence or absence of recruitment.

Huizing [102] includes the following symptoms in his list:

1. *High Threshold Discrimination for Pure Tone Audiometry*

Since the recruiting subject has a smaller difference limen, the margin between hearing and not hearing will be narrow and he thus responds to threshold tests with confidence.

2. *Sudden Decrease in Speech Reception Capacity*

A slight increase in threshold loss will bring about a loss in capacity to hear speech out of all proportion to the increase in deafness.

3. *Lack of Voice Control when Trying on a Hearing Aid for the First Time*

The explanation of this occurrence as a symptom of recruitment is as follows: The patient's voice, being near the microphone, is of higher intensity than that of the speaker some feet away, and this being so, recruitment may occur for the higher intensity but not for the lower, causing an "abnormally large" discrepancy between the loudness of the two voices. The sudden, unexpected loudness of the patient's own voice causes him to lose the normal control he has over his own voice and sometimes may cause a mental blockage which prevents him from speaking at all.

Mygrind [150] associates recruitment with *tinnitus* (ringing in the ears), diplacusis (hearing a sound of higher pitch in the recruiting ear than in the nonrecruiting ear), *low tolerance for loud sounds*, and *vertigo* (dizziness). Harbert and Sataloff [83] suggest similar symptoms, and also maintain that a *sound often appears distorted* to a recruiting subject—often complaining that voices or music sound "tinny," "fuzzy," or "hollow."

Harbert and Sataloff are in agreement with a number of

writers that recruiting subjects may have a lowered threshold of tolerance from those with normal ears. Liden [127] and Harold,[86] however, believe that a lowered threshold of discomfort does not necessarily accompany recruitment.

AETIOLOGY AND RECRUITMENT

The earlier workers in the field such as Steinberg and Gardner,[179] Fowler,[65] and Nilsson [153] were interested in the loudness balance test as a means of distinguishing between nerve and conductive deafnesses—the presence of recruitment indicating a nerve deafness and its absence a conductive deafness. They believed that the results of tuning fork tests and bone conduction audiometry were often misleading, particularly in cases of unilateral deafness or where there was considerable difference in acuity between the two ears, because of cross conduction.

Both Palva [157] and Littler [131] point out that before the work of Dix, Hallpike and Hood,[37] who in 1948 reported on the results of loudness balance tests given to thirty patients with Ménière's disease and twenty patients with deafness caused by degeneration of the eighth nerve owing to pressure of infiltration by tumours, it was generally believed that recruitment was present in all cases of nerve deafness. Dix, Hallpike and Hood found recruitment present and complete in all cases of Ménière's disease and completely absent in fourteen of the eighth nerve deafness cases with slight recruitment in the remaining six cases. They believe that recruitment was due to degeneration of the hair cells in the organ of Corti and that the loudness balance test can be used as a technique for distinguishing between deafness involving the cochlea, which will show recruitment, and deafness caused by the nerve involvement beyond the cochlea for which there will be no recruitment.[38] The slight recruitment displayed by some cases with deafness caused by disorders of the eighth nerve is explained in terms of secondary cochlea involvement caused by interference with cochlea blood supply.

Fowler [60] and Huizing [102] disagreed with the finding of Dix, Hallpike and Hood, that recruitment was characteristically absent in cases of deafness caused by retrocochlea lesions. The finding has, however, been confirmed by a large number of workers including Eby and Williams,[40] Lundberg [134] and Harold.[86] If, as seems likely, recruitment does occur only in the cochlea, the determination of its presence can be seen to represent a very useful aid to the diagnosis of various deafnesses.

RECRUITMENT AND HEARING FOR SPEECH

Finally, what effect does loudness recruitment have on a patient's hearing for speech? Until recently it was generally thought that it was detrimental. Harold found on examining the aetiologies of the cases used by previous workers, however, that a very large proportion were deaf as a result of *Ménière's disease*. Ménière's disease is a perceptive condition of adulthood and it has been well established that all such cases recruit and all hear speech badly. Harold contended therefore that this preponderance of Ménière's disease cases in each group gave the impression that all *recruiting* cases heard speech poorly. He found no significant difference between the hearing for speech of recruiting and nonrecruiting cases in the adult group, and in the children's group, those with recruitment heard speech significantly better than did the nonrecruiting ones.

Chapter 8

THE PROVISION OF AUDITORY EXPERIENCE

CARHART [17] CONSIDERED AN AWARENESS of sound could best be developed by surrounding the child with loud noises that were related to his everyday life. He recommended the use of games involving loud sound as the stimulus during this initial stage, to build up an enjoyment of auditory experience. The second step in Carhart's four stage auditory training programme was the development of gross discriminations. A set of noise makers was suggested: bell, drums, cymbals, automobile horns, etc. Stage 3 involved discriminations of simple speech patterns by contrasting vowels such as [a] and [i] either in isolation or in simple words. An alternative approach was tried in which meaningful phrases were introduced from the start, it being claimed that as the phrases became more familiar, the individual words would emerge. To accomplish the final stage in this programme—the finest possible discriminations of speech—Carhart recommended the acquisition of three skills: (a) the recognition of the more subtle phonetic differences in words; (b) the understanding of a large vocabulary, and (c) the following of connected speech.

To Whitehurst,[204] the term auditory training was synonymous with directed listening. She held that the most effective means of achieving this was through a carefully graded series of listening exercises which began with single words and progressed to complex patterns of speech.

Ronnei [168] wrote a manual of lessons to be used with individual children from six to eight years of age who were learning to use hearing aids. Listening, she maintained, was a complex function, the habit of which was acquired "through interest in, concentration on, and repetition of, satisfying (auditory) experiences." There were twenty-four carefully planned lessons in the scheme suggested. The first three of these concerned the discriminations of gross sounds. The next proceeded in graded steps from the most easily understood speech sounds, to those which were more difficult to hear and were not supplemented by guiding clues. All sounds were presented in words.

Huizing [101] recommended training the auditory function. He gave consideration to six factors: (a) The development of the discriminations of rhythmic patterns—a metronome was used in the beginning and developments included a variety of sounds against a musical background. Gymnastics, singing, and dancing, were all part of this section. (b) Practice in frequency discrimination. This was regarded as a principal factor in discriminating one voice from another. (c) The recognition of variations in intensity as an aid to the modulation of the child's own voice. (d) Raising of the threshold of tolerance (by about 10 db.) through listening to sound at loud levels. (e) Drills in the perception of various speech sounds. As far as possible, the material used for this should, he said, be meaningful to the child. (f) The "unconscious absorption" of all types of sound and through this process of functional rehabilitation, an adjustment to life's situations.

Wedenberg [198] devised a very interesting auditory training scheme which gave particular emphasis to the frequencies of speech sounds—especially the vowel formants. He considered that the order in which sounds should be presented to each child, could be determined by plotting the pure tone audiogram on a schematic drawing of the formant spectrum (Fig. 23) and assessing from this which sounds the child was likely to hear most readily. Such significance was placed on this that where children had been given names which contained mainly sounds of high frequency and low intensity (e.g., Chris and Stig), parents were encouraged to change them. Wedenberg also considered that hearing words should precede seeing them so that the children would become auditorily minded.

A useful book of practical listening games and exercises for use by parents and teachers of preschool children is that of Lowell and Stoner, *Play It By Ear.*[150] A manual produced by the Michigan School for Deaf Children (1959), *Auditory Training*, also contains a host of suggestions for teachers of school-aged children.

The perception of sound by profoundly deaf children was investigated by van Uden (Becking).[6] It was found that loud sounds were perceived not only auditorily but also kinaesthetically. In the main, sounds above 500 c.p.s. were heard, but sounds below this frequency were first detected as a vibration in the chest or legs. Upon this dual means of receiving sound, van Uden based his training programme [183] (to be described in some detail later).

The Ewings [52] describe an auditory approach in assisting children to read, to speak and, to comprehend language as well as to hear—(the *listening-reading-speaking method* or *LRS*). Essentially, it depends on the teacher first speaking close to the microphone of the hearing aid while pointing in a book to the words as they are said. Next, the child is asked to repeat the phrase or sentence while the teacher again points to the words. Success was claimed for this method when only ten minutes of individual practice was given daily. Further evidence supporting this is provided by John and Howarth [114] in a more recent research using this technique with twenty-nine severely and profoundly deaf children. A 56 per cent improvement in speech intelligibility was achieved by getting the children to reproduce the teacher's pattern as nearly as possible. The children concentrated on whatever auditory information they could perceive while watching as the teacher pointed to each syllable.

For many years at the Woodford School for Deaf Children in Essex,[103] and in an increasing number of classes in England, a similar technique to the above, has been used in a group situation (Fig. 37 a and b). Meaningful language material is written on the blackboard and the teacher, speaking close to the microphone of a group hearing aid, first reads the paragraph to the children at a near normal rate, while pointing to each word. The children listen and watch the blackboard rather than the teacher's face. Pictures, apparatus, and dramatisation are then used as required in the normal way to make the meaning clear. As the lesson develops, the teacher frequently asks the children to listen while she covers her mouth and says words or phrases for them. Another common auditory exercise at the end of the lesson is for the teacher to walk behind the class and whilst they watch the blackboard, to read a few words and stop. She then touches a child on the head and he is required to say the next word. It is remarkable that after regular daily practice, even most profoundly deaf children are able to do this. This technique is really very simple, and yet seems to be one of the most strikingly effective so far devised.

DEGREE OF DEAFNESS OF THE CHILDREN

The earlier writers, and Whitehurst, Ronnei and Huizing, make no reference to the hearing loss of the children for whom their programmes were designed. Huizing included four audiograms in his article, and the most severe hearing loss shown was 75 db. Ronnei has since stated that the children for whom her scheme was written had hearing losses in the better ear of not greater than 70 db. over the frequencies 300-400 c.p.s. Urbantschitsch, Goldstein, and Whitehurst included as exercises, discriminations between consonants. It is assumed, therefore, that

Figure 37A. The Listening-Reading-Speaking method applied with five year olds.

Figure 37B. The LRS method applied with older children.

their schemes were not written for children whose auditory impairments were in excess of about 80 db.

With the exception of Barczi and van Uden then, all writers had made provision for children with losses up to about 80 db. Barczi, the Ewings,[58] van Uden, had considered the range 80-95 db. Only Barczi, Hudgins and van Uden have described using the hearing of children whose losses exceeded 95 db.

It was found that even where writers had given numerical values to their classifications, definitions in terminology varied considerably. Van Uden categorized any child with a loss of less than 90 db. as hard of hearing. Hudgins' [93] classification (American Scale) was 50-65 hard of hearing, 65-80 partially deaf, greater than 80 db. profoundly deaf. The Ewings [58] considered children with hearing losses from 60-80 db. were severely deaf, and from 80-95 more severely deaf. Clarke [25] classified all children with losses between 75 and 95 db. as profoundly deaf. Thus in the limited range of hearing loss 75-80 db., children have been variously termed hard of hearing, partially deaf, severely deaf and pro-

foundly deaf. It is suggested that the use of such discrepant no-
menclature can create considerable confusion for students of this
subject.

The above review of literature is by no means comprehensive,
but it includes some of the more important approaches which
seem to have been helpful in providing deaf children with sound.
Two trends are evident: (a) graded listening exercises during
set periods each day or each week, and (b) the provision of sound
on as full-time a basis as is possible. It is also clear from the literature, that little scientific research has been attempted to show ob-
jectively that a particular method of auditory training was effective or superior to any other method. This may in part be due to
the absence of really precise measuring devices of speech reception or production—particularly for the more severely deaf children. The construction of such tests are urgently required.

It is realised that to give such individual auditory training
lessons in school time usually requires extra staffing and this is
not always easy to arrange. Parents can, and should, of course,
do much to direct their child's listening to all the interesting and
meaningful sounds which occur in and about the home, and
should use the LRS technique, referred to earlier, whenever possible.

The second approach, however, seems to have been accepted
by nearly all present day workers. The remainder of this chapter
is concerned with obtaining this intelligent full-time use of hearing aids by deaf children.

THE FULL TIME USE OF HEARING AIDS

Individual aids should be worn in much the same way as many
people wear spectacles, i.e., they are the first thing they grope for
in the morning and the last thing they take off at night. Children
wearing aids should learn to put them on as soon as they have had
a wash in the morning and should leave them on—as far as possible—until bedtime at night. Obviously, when swimming, bath-
ing or playing boisterous games, aids must be removed, but at
nearly all other times, they should be worn. In very noisy conditions if wearing the aid becomes too unpleasant, they should
switch them off rather than *take* them off. Adults will sometimes

put the aid on to listen to the radio, remove it while they read a book, put it on again because a visitor has called, take it off to have a meal and so on. Children, too, will often remove the aids because it is an arithmetic lesson or a silent reading lesson. Children or adults who are continually putting their hearing aids on and taking them off, however, rarely make any real use of them. They are really just fooling with the aid. "Put them on and forget them" should be the maxim. If the aids are worn comfortably, as will be emphasised later, it is not uncommon for wearers to comment that throughout the day they only remember that they have the aid on once or twice.

Whilst no prosthetic device is popular with children, it should be realised that hearing aids are very much less popular than are spectacles. Late in 1957, 289 normally hearing children (178 boys and 111 girls) in Manchester city schools were asked the following questions: "If you had to wear one of the following, which would you prefer and why?—a hearing aid, spectacles, or a brace on a leg." Two hundred seventeen of the 289 children (approximately 75 per cent) preferred spectacles to the other two devices. Fourteen of the boys and twenty-one of the girls chose hearing aids because they believed the modern ones could not be seen. In effect then, no one would know they were using a hearing aid at all. If these thirty-five children are subtracted from both groups, the very definite prejudice against the hearing aid and the caliper is even more pronounced. With this adjustment, approximately 85 per cent of the children preferred spectacles (79 per cent of the boys and 98 per cent of the girls).

Some of the reasons for the preference of spectacles revealed the stigma which according to these children was attached to hearing aids and leg calipers. "People don't think of you as though there is something seriously wrong." "It is nothing to be ashamed of." "The other two are unsightly . . . ugly." "With a hearing aid you get called names." One boy chose a brace on a leg because "If I wore the other two, people would laugh at me."

There is one important exception to the rule of the fullest use of aids, and that is that very shy boys should not be pressed to wear hearing aids in the streets, in buses, and so on, if they state that they do not wish to do so. The reason for this is that whereas the girls can conceal their hearing aids completely by allowing their hair to cover the cord and ear mould, with boys, this is not possible. Occasionally, parents argue that they feel the hearing aids should be worn conspicuously so that strangers can see immediately that they have a hearing loss and can make suitable allowances for them. While there is some virtue in this the disadvantage of the unnecessary attention by curious members of the public which the hearing aids direct to deaf children seems well to outweigh it. Fifty years ago, I understand spectacles were not at all popular and it was not uncommon for someone at the theatre to slip his spectacles on after the lights went off and to remove them (if possible) just before the lights came on again. No one stares at a little boy wearing glasses these days, but in bus queues, in shops and in buses, they still do take some long looks at children with hearing aids.

Early Fitting. The secret of obtaining ready acceptance of hearing aids is to fit the children as early as possible in life. The hearing aid then becomes so much a part of them, that they wear them as readily as they do their shoes and socks. In Australia, where the Commonwealth Acoustic Laboratories have been issuing aids to children from about the age of two years, it has been found that they are worn quite unselfconsciously even throughout the adolescent period.

In April, 1957, twenty-five children who had been issued with hearing aids and who were attending ordinary schools in a city area were seen in clinic sessions. Incidentally, no less than five of these were found on examination to be not sufficiently deaf to wear hearing aids, and were recommended to discontinue using them. The fifteen deafest children of the remaining twenty were formed into a research group in an effort to try and get them to wear their hearing aids regularly. When first seen, only four of these fifteen children were wearing their hearing aids all the time *in school* and none was wearing his or her aid either *at home* or *out of school*. At the end of seven months, however, eleven of the fifteen children were wearing their hearing aids all the time *in school* and *at home*, and seven wore them all the time *out of school*.

PROCEDURES HELPFUL IN SECURING REGULAR USE
OF HEARING AIDS

Adult Interest

Unless at least one adult will take an interest in the hearing aid, it will very rarely be worn. It seems that the more adults there are who will give the child some encouragement, the easier it is for him and the more likelihood there is of his wearing it continuously. Parents, teachers, the hearing aid technicians, the family doctor, brothers and sisters, aunts and uncles and so on, can all help here. The doctors and aunts, etc., need only say to the child, "How is the hearing aid going?" It is often a good talking point to begin a conversation with a deaf child if one has not seen him before or if one sees him infrequently, and it certainly helps the child to feel that all sorts of people are pleased to see him wearing the aid.

In schools and classes for deaf children, it is *essential* that the *senior teachers* and the *class teachers* recognise the value of hearing aids and give active encouragement to the children and do not just pay lipservice to the idea of the full-time use of hearing aids. Getting deaf children to wear hearing aids is rather like a mathematics or a speech scheme in a school—if the principal is not prepared to put his or her weight into seeing that the programme is carefully launched and conscientiously carried out, everyone's task is made much more difficult. The first thing a sceptical headmaster or teacher might do is to take some of the simple tests described in this book and experiment carefully with a number of children until he convinces himself of the fact that sound does mean something to almost every child.

The principal and teachers should aim at enabling the children to make the most intelligent use of hearing aids in conditions which approximate as nearly as possible to the optimum. The correct attitude to hearing aids makes a real difference to one's work with them. Tasks such as changing a discharged battery or a broken lead which were previously regarded as "additional chores placed on the shoulders of an already overworked teacher," become just as necessary as marking a child's work or correcting a poorly pronounced word. If one regards sound as almost as important as food to a deaf child, it helps one get such factors as the time and money spent on the equipment in perspective.

Class teachers have a responsibility to check the performance of individual hearing aids. This serves the dual purpose (a) of ensuring that all aids are performing satisfactorily and (b) of showing the children that the teacher is genuinely interested in their aids. With most nursery and infant school children, checking should be done twice each day and with older children, once a day. "Am I to spend half my day fiddling about with hearing aids then?" says the harassed teacher. The answer is "No, the average time for little children is seven to eight minutes a day and for the older ones three minutes." It may be added that even this time is not wasted since it presents a good opportunity for pertinent and meaningful language work.

One method of checking the hearing aid performance which has proved quite effective is the following:

1. (Children stand around the teacher in a semi-circle) "Switch your hearing aids off."

2. "Take the ear mould out." Children remove moulds and hold them about nine inches from the microphone of the hearing aid.

3. "John," (1st child) "switch your hearing aid on." The boy turns his volume control to maximum. The teacher listens for about two seconds to hear that there is a strong clear whistling noise (acoustic feedback). If this is so, the child is told to switch it off and the second one switches on. This goes on until all the hearing aids have been tested. Any faulty aids are then dealt with.

It may, of course, be necessary to teach the class the words which are being used and demonstrate exactly how each step is to be performed. The procedure may seem somewhat "military" but the checking can take a long time if one is not careful and complications such as two hearing aids being switched on at the same time can cause confusion unless one has the class under strict control. Checking should be "snappy." The use of a watch soon gives the children this idea. Daily times can be recorded on the blackboard for a number of weeks.

By using the above method with a class of nine children ten

years of age, the time of checking during a four week period ranged between one-half minute and ten minutes—the average being three minutes. One must guard against checking aids each day for a week and upon finding no faults at all (as is possible sometimes) presuming that such regular attention is unnecessary. The teacher of the above class, for example, was absent from school for a week and the children were allocated to classes where aids were not being checked. At the beginning of the following week, fifteen minutes on the first day and thirty minutes on the second were spent in getting all the hearing aids in order. In the long run time is saved by checking the aids every day.

When aids are worn regularly both indoors and outside, breakages and faults must be expected in addition to the replacement of spent batteries. In a day and residential nursery school and a residential school for children aged from seven to seventeen years, hearing aids were being worn very conscientiously.

An analysis of the replacements required in these schools over a one year period provides norms (though very approximate) which indicate what may be expected (Table 6).

Upon analysis, the figures in Table 6 show that in the nursery school the average number of replacements for the year was approximately forty-one per child, i.e., roughly one fault found each school week. With the older children, however, a considerable reduction in breakages is evident and the average number of replacements is approximately twenty-five per child—or a little more than one each fortnight. The cost per annum to schools of running the hearing aids was approximately £6 for the nursery school and £2 10 for the older group.

Despite much care on the part of a staff, many of the replacements in a nursery school are caused by misuse rather than normal wear. The youngest children frequently chew the cords until they break, and a number of the receivers and moulds are lost (particularly in long grass) rather than broken, during play out of doors. The children must also be discouraged from twirling the mould and receiver on the end of the cord, which frequently results in damage or loss if the receiver flies off the lead terminals. A sudden "craze" such as this, may result in the loss of seven or eight moulds and receivers in one afternoon. Careful supervision

TABLE 6

REPLACEMENTS REQUIRED FOR INDIVIDUAL HEARING AIDS IN TWO
SCHOOLS FOR DEAF CHILDREN DURING A ONE YEAR PERIOD

Replacement	Nursery School (25 children – aged 3 – 7 years)	Residential School (300 children – aged 7 + years)
Batteries	818	7,234
Leads (cords)	143	170
Receivers	28	12
Output blocks	22	—
Volume controls	8	30
Switch arms	7	—
Microphone contacts	5	20
Listening coils	—	15
Miscellaneous	7	3
	1,038	7,484

of children by competent staff may be said to be necessary in
every school, but when little children wear hearing aids out of
doors, such provision is absolutely essential. On one occasion
when twelve monopack hearing aids were issued to a residential
nursery school without first ensuring that staff were competent
to supervise their use, within eight days only two of the aids were
performing satisfactorily. On inspection, six were found to have
been left switched on when removed by the children at night, one
receiver had been broken and another lost, one lead had been
chewed through, and the battery terminals of one aid were not
making adequate contact.

Parents and *supervisors* must also be given instruction in the
use of hearing aids. The greater their knowledge of the subject
the better. Principals and class teachers have a responsibility
here to ensure that such information is given to them. In addition to a certain amount of theory, both the parents and "substi-
tute parents" need to be given demonstrations of what each child
is able to hear, with, and without, his hearing aid, and they should
be able to check the performance of a hearing aid and do the
elementary maintenance.

They should also know the best setting for each child's volume
control. If parents realise that during the holidays the sole responsibility for the child wearing his hearing aid rests with them,

they will have a stock of batteries and a cord and receiver on hand in the event of breakages.

Supervisors are best to check the hearing aids of the little children at night, (a) to see that they are working, and (b) to ensure that they have been switched off. It is unwise to leave the hearing aids of these young children beside their beds, since they find them interesting playthings when they wake early. Aids should be placed out of sight and reach, each night, and distributed each morning.

In conclusion, then, it is re-emphasized that the more interest that can be shown in the hearing aids by adults, the more likelihood there is of a child using his aid sensibly at all times.

Child Interest and Participation

The aim is that, as soon as possible, the children will become intelligent and discriminating users of hearing aids. They should report faults in the aids as soon as they occur, though very deaf children often have difficulty in doing this. If encouraged, they will inform parents and teachers of the various things they can hear when wearing the aid. As they become older they should be capable of looking after the hearing aid by themselves.

Whilst bearing in mind that to begin with at least, a hearing aid is often something that a deaf child *needs* but doesn't *want*, there are several ways which have proved very helpful in showing them that the aid is of benefit to them, and in consequence to convince them of the value of wearing it. The first is by means of *speech tests*. For example, if a boy hears 60 per cent of the words in a word list correctly, when using the aid, and only 30 per cent without it, one can then show him the scores and say, "You see the hearing aid is useful, isn't it?" Similarly, with profoundly deaf children after using the paired vowel test, they often realise that they have some discrimination of speech sounds with the aid but cannot even hear the sound of voice unaided. With older children, this semi-scientific approach seems a good one.

Secondly, and perhaps the best possible way, is if the children can be given pleasurable *listening experiences* through the aids. Statements like the following which refer to three partially hearing children who had been recently given aids show that they were convinced of their value.

> A boy aged fourteen years with a hearing loss of 45 db. said, "I wore my hearing aid in the park and for the first time I heard the birds whistle.
> "In the pictures I can hear much better and it will not take long for me to make out every word they say."
> A girl aged fifteen years with a hearing loss of 40 db.— "Hearing much better with it. My voice dropped lower. It's better for people who speak to me."
> A ten-year-old girl with a hearing loss of 53 db. whose mother wrote, "Asked on the first day, 'Is it really necessary for me to wear it, as I can hear just as well without it?' On the second day, 'If I turn the volume up it whistles—if I turn it up only a little it makes no difference.' On the third day she arrived home all smiles, saying she managed it all right and it makes a differences."

It seemed that at one stage during the third day this girl had perhaps been listening to her teacher and realised she was understanding what was being said better than ever before.

> An eight-year-old girl with a hearing loss of 80 db. said when I visited her home recently, "Wait a minute. I am deaf," and went off to get her hearing aid.
> Similarly, statements by very deaf people like Mrs. M. that the hearing aid had "made life more interesting" or of the Dutch girl who on removing the aid said, "Now I am alone again" are further evidence that the wearers realise that things are better with the aid than without it.

Knowledge about hearing aids can be helpful; their performance, the best conditions for using them, the best way to wear them and the general management of them. Ewing and Ewing [58] have given useful suggestions in this connection (*ibid*, Chapter XIII).

The *need for hearing aids* should be created. It is clear that if children are in residential schools where the free use of signs and gestures accompany their almost silent lip movements they do not feel the need for using what hearing they have since they can understand one another quite adequately without the use of sound. Justman and Moskowitz,[117] for example, noted that when the deaf children in their study began attending ordinary school classes for part of each day, they soon became much more conscious of the value of their hearing aids and would report breakages promptly although they had never bothered to do this before. (The better use of hearing aids thus becomes one more reason why deaf children should spend as much time as possible surrounded by those who hear normally.)

Integrating with talking people is one good way to show deaf children the advantages of wearing aids, but teachers and parents should see that opportunities arise as often as possible for the children to use what hearing they have—visits to orchestras, to short concerts, to films, to car races, to farmyards, etc., should all be more interesting and meaningful to most deaf children if they are wearing their aids (and the aid is working properly!). The children's attention should also, of course, be directed to meaningful sounds in their everyday environment—the radio or television, noises made when preparing food, cleaning the house, at meal times, when gardening or working with tools outside and so on.

Finally with older children who definitely do hear speech better aided than unaided, it is often possible to emphasize to them that in addition to it being easier for them to understand speakers it is easier for the people *who talk to them* if they wear aids. One can tell such children that people get tired of saying everything to them two or three times over, and that it is so much easier and nicer if one can talk more normally to them.

How the Hearing Aid is Worn on the Person

The way in which the child wears the hearing aid may at first seem too trivial a point to require discussion. With experience, however, it soon becomes clear that this factor can be critical to the success or failure of any auditory rehabilitation programme. *The aim should be to wear the hearing aids as comfortably and as inconspicuously as possible whilst still enabling them to perform at maximum.*

There is no one way to wear a hearing aid, but the following are suggestions. For children up to about the age of seven years, some form of *harness* seems necessary. Certain features should be incorporated in this:

1. It should be made of some strong type of material. Flimsy cotton harnesses are inclined to crease and crumple up so that quite soon they will not lie flat.

2. It should be easy to put on and remove. As little time as possible should be taken dressing and undressing the children in their harness and quite soon they should be able to manage their own.

3. It should be adjustable so that the aid can be kept firm on the child no matter what he or she is wearing.

4. A small pocket should be sewn on to one shoulder strap of the harness just large enough to accommodate the child's ear mould and receiver. When the aid is not in use or is removed for the night, these can be placed in the pockets, and no harm comes to them. If left loose, the children play with them and/or they drop on the floor during individual lessons with the speech training aid. When the aids are hung up at night, the receivers can bang against the wall and frequently the bakelite backs are broken.

5. There should also be a pocket sewn on the front which should:

    a. Be just large enough to hold the child's hearing aid and a piece of stiff backing material, e.g., corrugated cardboard.

    b. The backing material should protrude about one-third inch above the hearing aid—it then serves the useful function of protecting the delicate controls at the top of the aid.

    c. Have a button-over flap at the top. This prevents food and liquids from entering the hearing aid, and prevents the aid from slipping out. Many a good hearing aid has ceased to perform as a result of slipping out into a handbasin or a toilet, or through becoming choked with milk or codliver oil. Button-over flaps prevent such occurrences.

    d. The flap should have the sides cut away so that the on-off switch and the volume control can be seen by the teacher or parent without having to half undress the child to ascertain whether the controls are in their correct position.

e. There should be a hole cut in the front of the pocket so that the microphone is not unnecessarily covered. A certain amount of covering over microphones is possible without affecting intelligibility unduly, e.g., a cardigan or jersey has no appreciable effect, nor has two or even three layers of a cotton material. A jersey plus a jacket, however, is likely to cause some interference, and so is a layer of the canvas material of which the pocket may be made.

f. In some hearing aids where *clothes rub* is a problem, the pocket may be lined with suede or silk and this is often helpful.

g. A button hole should be cut in the flap of the pocket directly above the cord socket. The cord can then be passed through this, through the shirt or blouse buttonhole, under the collar of the garment and up to the earpiece.

6. The hearing aid should be worn high on the chest. When it is placed lower down, damage soon results as little children roll on the floor or use climbing or tumbling apparatus. The disadvantage of wearing the aids high on the chest is that this brings the microphone closer to the receiver and there is thus more likelihood of acoustic feedback resulting. It is felt, however, that an aid which "whistles" a little at times is better than one which doesn't work at all. Suggestions are made in the next section, "Maintenance and Servicing of Aids," on some procedures which help eliminate acoustic feedback.

Older Children. From about seven years of age, and often earlier, harnesses can be dispensed with, and a large proportion of the older children manage by clipping their hearing aids to a pocket in a shirt, blouse or frock, or to the underclothes. Others wear a braid around their necks which takes the weight of the aid, and some use a cord tied around the body to which the aid is attached.

One method which satisfies the condition of being "comfortable" and "inconspicuous," etc., is the following: The hearing aid is placed in the top pocket of the shirt or blouse, which is not so loose that the aid bangs about when the child runs. A top is sewn on the pocket to keep the aid from bouncing out. A button-hole is cut at the back of the pocket just behind the cord plug. The cord is then passed through this button-hole and up under the collar, behind the child's ear and plugs into the receiver (Fig. 38). Girls are encouraged to grow hair over their ears and thus conceal the hearing aid completely. If it is desired, a loop

Figure 38. Older child wearing a hearing aid.

of tape can be sewn on to the back collar of the garment and the cord, when passed through this, cannot slip around to the side and become visible.

Avoid the "festoon" effect with the cord so frequently adopted by hearing aid users. Cords should be worn close to the body and as far as possible, kept out of sight. Young children chew them if given the opportunity and all children get them caught in things as they play if they are dangling loose. A further advantage of wearing them *under* clothing is that it makes the aids more difficult to get off, and thus this frequently deters the older children from removing them five or six times during the day.

Maintenance and Elementary Servicing of Aids

The efficient maintenance and servicing of hearing aid equipment is a necessity. Few things deter a child more than to have his aid develop a fault and then to have to wait weeks before it is returned to him. Teachers, too, can lose interest in a hearing programme if three or four of the children in the class are without aids.

The following are some suggestions for maintaining aids in good order:

1. If using government hearing aids, as for example, in Great Britain, Australia and New Zealand, an officer from the hearing aid clinic should make regular visits to the school or unit as often as is necessary, to collect defective aids, to return mended ones, to take ear impressions, and to discuss points with both teachers and children. A good technician can give much encouragement to children, teachers and principals.

2. One teacher who is particularly interested should be responsible for the hearing aids, and a record of aids and replacements issued should be kept by him. This person should have a stock of spares which includes batteries (kept at a temperature of 70° F.), cords, receivers and temporary ear moulds. He should also possess a reserve of about ten hearing aids for every one hundred children in the school to be lent to children whose own hearing aids develop faults and are required to be sent away. It is important to have such a stock of aids before any serious hear-

ing aid programme is begun. The teacher responsible for aids
(if not every teacher), should possess a small battery tester.

3. Apart from seeing that aids are properly worn and checking their performance in class daily, class teachers should locate
faults when aids are not working properly. Faults may be found
by a process of elimination. The following steps are suggested:

a. See that *the hearing aid controls are in their correct
position*, e.g., the aid is not switched on to the induction loop
system, the volume control is at maximum, etc.

b. *Batteries.* As could be seen from Table 6, by far the
commonest cause of difficulty with aids results from discharged batteries. Replace the battery with a new one. If
this does not eliminate the fault, then check:

c. *Battery Terminals.* At either end of the battery compartment there is a small metal clip. If these become bent or
are covered with a greenish verdigris, the battery cannot make
proper contact. These terminals may be cleaned with a piece
of fine glass paper or bent back into position with a pen knife
or sometimes a small Yale type key. Such faults are not very
frequent, but whilst one has the battery compartment open it
is as well to check them.

d. Next check the *lead*. Leads (or cords) are expensive
items which can give a great deal of bother even when aids
are worn correctly. The nursery school quoted above (Table
6) spent £40 1 3d. in one year on batteries, and £40 17 6
during the same period on leads. When the tiny wires in the
cord are broken, every now and again they touch, completing
the circuit and the aid feeds back for a short time. Such aids
are said to be *intermittent*. Faults in leads can often be located by placing the hearing aid on a table with the receiver
near the microphone and then wiggling the lead particularly
at either end near the plugs, where breakages most frequently
occur. One should also be sure that the points of the plugs are
clean (shiny) and are fitting firmly into their sockets. They
may also be cleaned with fine glass paper. Replace the lead
with a new one.

e. *The Ear Mould.* Check that the canal of the ear mould

is not blocked with grease or some other obstruction. Pipe cleaners, needles or fine wire can be used for this. Children should learn to clean ear moulds every night. The moulds should be rubbed with a piece of cloth or tissue paper. They should not be washed in warm soapy water as is commonly done, as this removes the fine glossy surface from the acrylic material of which they are made.

f. Finally, check *the receiver*, by replacing it with a new one. Receivers need rather more care than many people realise. (They are more expensive than many realise also— about 2 guineas for a receiver of good quality.)

g. If the fault has not been located after these points have been checked it is likely to be an internal one which requires the aid to be returned to the hearing aid clinic or the retailer who supplied it, for servicing.

Preferably a short course of instruction, but certainly some written information about hearing aids which has been related to their child, should be given to parents *before* they are asked to accept responsibility for the hearing aid when the child is at home. They should, also, be given a few batteries and a spare cord or so.

ACOUSTIC FEEDBACK

When very deaf children are asked to wear hearing aids, one is sometimes bedevilled by *acoustic feedback*. This is the whistling sound which results when a very quiet sound which comes from the receiver of a hearing aid is picked up by the microphone, amplified, and put out (slightly louder), at the receiver again. It is then picked up by the microphone again and amplified further. It can be caused by: (a) leakage of this sound *round the mould*; (b) leakage between the mould and the receiver, i.e., when the ring and spring fitting is not giving a complete seal off of the sound, and (c) leakage from the plug socket of the hearing aid cord. It will be appreciated that feedback is more likely to occur when hearing aids are being run near their maximum output. It is thus with the deafer children that most difficulty is encountered.

The solution to the problem is not simply to ignore the whistling sound and carry on as though it was not present. Children who wear aids when they are feeding back, cannot hear at all well with them—they are better advised to remove them altogether than to persist with them if the whistling cannot be stopped.

Feedback round the mould is best detected by simply placing the ball of the thumb firmly over the end of the canal of the mould while keeping the microphone at least nine inches away from the receiver. If the feedback ceases, it can be assumed that it was due to leakage round the mould.

(*a*) This is easily the most common cause of acoustic feedback. Very often it is the result of a poorly fitting ear mould. "*A mould is only as good as the impression from which it was made.*" Modern techniques and impressioning materials have largely overcome this problem.[158a] Ill-fitting moulds can, of course, cause much discomfort to the wearer whether feedback is present or not. Teachers and parents of little children should watch carefully for any signs of this.

Be sure the mould is fitting snugly in the child's ear.

If it appears to be fitting well but still feeds back, some *silicone grease* can be applied to seal off the tiny gaps between the mould and the ear. This is a useful temporary measure until another impression can be taken.

Feedback can also be reduced by eliminating peaky responses in receivers.

With little children, if the ear mould tends to drop out, a small plastic button can be stuck to the back of the receiver with a piece of pink plastic coated wire attached. This can be bent so that it hooks over the ear and thus helps keep the mould in place.

(*b*) *Feedback Between Ear Mould and Receiver.* If the feedback is found not to be round the mould, the ear mould should be detached and the thumb applied firmly to the ring aperture of the receiver. If the feedback then ceases, it is likely that the fault is located at the ring and spring connection. This can be packed with two or three plastic washers or washers made of binding cloth or even blotting paper. It is worthwhile trying one or two different receivers to try and obtain a better fit if the washers are not effective. Sometimes it is necessary to have a new mould made. Feedback between mould and receiver can, of course, occur if the canal of the mould is blocked with wax.

(c) *Feedback from the Lead Plug.* When the sockets which hold the lead plug in the receiver become worn, a gap frequently occurs between the plug and the receiver and leakage of sound from this can cause feedback. Any good cement will keep the plug from slipping and usually prevent sound leakages. Sometimes Cellotape can be used for this.

(d) *Feedback Through the Receiver.* Nearly all receivers will feed back through the bakelite at the back, if the hearing aid microphone is placed very close to them. Very occasionally a defective receiver feeds back from a considerable distance. If when used by a child who requires only slight amplification the receiver still feeds back, then it should not be accepted and a new one supplied.

All hearing aids will feed back less if some obstruction is placed in a direct line between the microphone and the receiver. For this reason it is useful sometimes to place the microphone compartment on the opposite side of the body from the ear in which the ear phone is placed. In this way, the chin of the wearer provides the obstruction to the sound and very frequently causes a reduction in acoustic feedback.

To enable children to wear hearing aids regularly is costly and it requires time and effort on the part of the adults who care for the children. The fact that in many schools children are wearing their hearing aids properly, however, shows that it is a realisable aim for every school.

MUSIC FOR DEAF CHILDREN

Music can be perceived by deaf children; they can derive tremendous pleasure from it; and the educational implications of it are considerable. For this reason no publication on the use of sound by deaf children would be complete without reference to music. Whilst recognising its value, my own experience in this field has not been extensive.

It is generally known that hearing for the low pitched tones is usually better than that for the higher ones. Nearly all deaf children, for example, have measurable hearing at 250 c.p.s., and below this frequency. Very many have hearing also up to 500 c.p.s. Middle C on the piano has a fundamental frequency of 256 c.p.s. The C below this has a main frequency of 128 c.p.s., and the one above middle C of 512 cycles. It is seen then, that the *melodies* of many tunes are able to be heard by very many "deaf" people, provided they are produced loudly enough (see Fig. 15).

It is important to stress that although the melody can often be heard quite clearly, the harmonics can not—similarly the voice of the singer can be clearly heard but the words he or she sings can never be intelligible to these very deaf children. It is interesting to listen to speech or to singing when the high frequency sounds have been cut out, i.e., low pass filters have been incorporated in the speech circuit at, say, 500 c.p.s. The vowels are all quite audible, but all sound rather like [ɜ] or [ʊ], and the consonants, if they are audible at all, sound like an indefinite breathy type of fricative. The voice takes on much of the quality of a deaf person's speech, except that there is more pitch modulation. Hudgins [159] found that the vowel sounds produced by deaf children all tended towards the neutral [ɜ] sound as in *bird*. We are reminded once again that "we speak very largely as we hear."

Presenting the Sound of Music to Deaf Children

For children with less severe hearing losses—say up to 70 db. —it seems possible to use very similar methods to those employed with normally hearing children. They are able to sing in a group, to play a variety of instruments and so on. It is very necessary, of course, that they wear their hearing aids for this.

For the severely and profoundly deaf children, instruments like recorders and pianos have been found not to produce the most audible sounds—the recorders seem too weak and the notes on the piano when struck, do not perseverate long enough. Some pianos seem better than others. The children stand round and feel the vibration by touching it. Unless some amplification is used, however, the deaf children are not able to hear the piano music so well. Easily the best instrument for deaf children to hear is the organ. Organs are made, of course, in a variety of shapes and sizes. The one shown in Figure 39 is a wind instrument produced in Holland after much experimentation. The specifica-

Figure 39. Small wind instrument in use.

tions were given by Father A. van Uden of the Instituut voor Doven, St. Michiels Gestel, Holland, who is probably the world authority on music for very deaf children.

In operation air pressure is built up in the reed chamber when the child blows down a small rubber pipe (Fig. 39). As each key is depressed, the appropriate reed is set in vibration. The sound from this is picked up by a microphone which is set in the lid of the reed box, and is relayed to an amplifier and then to the child's earphones. These are extremely useful little instruments, since profoundly deaf children can begin playing them when only four or five years of age, and when fourteen or fifteen years old they still enjoy using them. These organs have a range of two octaves above middle C, and a maximum output of 120 db., above .0002 dynes/cm², with a flat response over all frequencies.

One objection to this type of organ is that it is not possible to include the octaves below middle C because the lower reeds become increasingly difficult to vibrate. This is unfortunate since the children usually hear this range well. If using an electronic organ rather than a wind one, it would of course be possible to use the lowest notes, but the children would then not have the practice of blowing and exercising the breath control which van Uden and others consider very valuable.

The teacher uses a small electrically operated Hohner organ (Fig. 40), which is connected to the children's amplifiers so that they can hear and copy the patterns given by the teacher if necessary.

Another main piece of equipment used by van Uden, is a battery of loudspeakers to which the organ, or a tape recorder, may be connected. Six twelve-inch conical speakers have been set in a baffle board. Van Uden and Becking[6] had found earlier that

Figure 40. The use of wind instruments by older children.

when wearing hearing aids, profoundly deaf children perceived sounds above 500 c.p.s., auditorily, but sounds below this were perceived as vibration on the body. A seventh speaker has therefore been placed in the bottom of a tall wooden box which has a "V" cut in the front and stands about five feet high. This speaker was specially constructed to give emphasis to low pitched sounds —below 500 c.p.s.

It is not of course essential to have the equipment exactly like that which has been described. Three loudspeakers placed at the back of the stage will give quite a good effect. In another school, two large speakers set in wooden cabinets of the "Karlson" type, have proved quite effective in a small room.

A bass-voiced singer with organ accompaniment seems to be one of the best combinations for presenting music to children with defective hearing. This can be tape recorded and played through amplifying systems such as those described above as well as through induction loops.

USE OF THE AMPLIFYING EQUIPMENT

With the nursery and infant groups, the emphasis is on the enjoyment of experiencing sound and developing an awareness to it by activities and exercises which involve hearing and feeling vibrations. Activity methods are used as much as possible, and perhaps 30 per cent of any lesson is devoted to developing physical skills and rhythmical movement where sound perception is not particularly stressed. The following are observations made during a lesson with four- to five-year-old children.

1. Children, on entering the room, ran to the wind instruments, opened them, put on the head sets, turned up the volume controls and began to play.

2. Two to three minutes were allowed for free play.

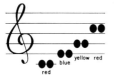

3. Sight reading from the blackboard.

Teacher pointed to "doh" on the blackboard and both she and the class teacher checked that the children found the correct note.

4. Played slowly up the scale as the teacher pointed to each pair of notes—class teacher checking carefully.

5. Playing notes selected at random by the teacher.

6. Relating notes to words:

(a) Played first as teacher pointed to them.

(b) Names were written in and teacher and children said the names as they played them. (Teacher using the Hohner organ.)

(c) Other names were thought of. Teacher added them to the others as above.

7. Children removed their head sets etc., and went to sit on a Swedish bench under the loudspeakers—shoes removed and individual aids put on.

8. Teacher demonstrated sitting on a chair with feet extended, then kicking rapidly in time with a series of middle C notes played on the Hohner organ.

9. After demonstration by the teacher, children began striding to each note sounded through the loudspeakers—doh Pause doh Pause, etc. At a continuous note, all ran back to the form. Repeated.

10. Repeated individually or in pairs—the teachers taking note which children were having difficulty. There were only three children of the twelve who seemed at all uncertain.

11. In a circle—striding round to doh, Pause, doh, Pause, etc. Changed to galloping when music changed to doh-doh, doh-doh, doh-doh, etc. Stopped when the music stopped. Repeated several times. At continuous sound, ran to the form once more.

12. Lesson ended with physical education activities, climbing on wall bars and forward and backward rolls on a gym-mat. Allocation of time: 1. Wind organs approximately ten minutes; 2. Loud speakers approximately ten minutes; 3. Physical education approximately ten minutes.

It will be noted that the approach adopted when the loudspeakers were used is very similar to that which is used in many nursery schools where rhythmic work is done—i.e., identification of various rhythms: walking, skipping, running, galloping, etc. The only difference, however, is that by using the loudspeakers as well as the induction coil, the children are able to perceive the music so much more clearly than when only a piano or a tape-recorder is used.

With older girls, the emphasis is placed on finer discriminations of pitch, rhythm, and the length of notes, words and phrases, and a more subtle application of this in speech, in ballet and interpretative dancing.

One period each week is spent playing the wind instruments, and the second period is devoted to dancing. Variety of presentation of material heightens the interest and enjoyment of the work. The following is one way in which a "play song" was presented with 10-year-old children over several weeks.

1. The words of the song were taught in class as a language lesson (and revised again by the specialist teacher).

2. The words were drilled in speech periods by the class teacher. One of the methods adopted for speech work in the senior school may be summarised as follows: (a) words are written under a blank staff; (b) syllables are marked; (c) approximate pitches of syllables are marked; (d) syllabic length is shown by musical notation.

3. Play on the wind instruments.

4. Compare this pattern with the music of the song.

5. Play the music of the song several times on the wind organs.

6. Revise speech in class.

7. Revision of the tune—played from a tape recorder through both the bank of speakers and the low frequency speaker—children listening and feeling the tune as they watch the specialist teacher point to the different notes.

8. Language is again discussed and from each phrase the actions of the dance are built up. The movements are a combination of conventional ballet steps and of interpretative dancing, which the children love to devise for themselves.

While the value to children of music and free rhythmical movement are self evident, the work has other extremely important aspects. Learning the words of the songs and pieces is good practice for reading, extends the children's vocabularies and their interest and knowledge of other people and countries. The words also provide interesting and useful material for speech improvement work. Making up play-songs and participating in them is great fun for deaf children, and is very good psychologically for them. Many of the songs, nursery rhymes, dances and stories they deal with will be known to their parents and their normally hearing brothers and sisters. These musical activities give excellent opportunities for them to express emotions and ideas in mime, when many of them have considerable difficulty to do this in words. Joy and grief, anger and compassion, weariness and energy, etc., can all be expressed so easily and subtly.

Finally, the use of musical notations to show length (which is of course closely related to strength) of the various syllables, and to help in pitch modulation is most effective when practice is given regularly. If the children hear the words played over first, each syllable being given its correct length, it can have a marked effect on the rate of their utterance and the phrasing and rhythm of their own speech, and makes for greater intelligibility.

APPENDIX 1

R.N.I.D. HEARING TEST CARDS

Card 1	cup	duck	jug	bus
Card 2	egg	peg	hen	bed
Card 3	cap	fan	cat	lamb
Card 4	key	feet	sheep	tree
Card 5	dog	cot	doll	sock
Card 6	knife	pie	pipe	kite

APPENDIX 2

M/J WORDS (SLIGHTLY ADAPTED)

List 1	List 2	List 3	List 4
A. car	F. ship	K. hand	P. look
bird	home	white	feet
school	cup	duck	chair
come	made	bed	road
play	egg	doll	egg
B. duck	G. day	L. car	Q. ship
bed	fish	mice	horse
broom	book	frog	bus
pig	ball	door	cow
doll	shoe	moon	black
C. four	H. horse	M. four	R. cup
shop	night	bird	long
hand	black	mat	day
man	feet	shop	girl
frog	man	play	night
D. sat	I. hat	N. come	S. hat
green	bus	fat	home
door	long	school	boat
white	chair	get	fish
mice	boat	green	shoe
E. cat	J. three	O. gun	T. three
gun	road	pig	jump
brown	girl	wood	man
wet	cow	cat	ball
wood	jump	brown	made

List 5	List 6	List 7	List 8
A. bad	F. book	K. with	P. good
dish	kind	put	room
sleep	train	milk	fast
milk	fast	car	one
boy	good	down	ball
B. run	G. pot	L. bad	Q. pot
fall	floor	fall	kind
house	meat	dog	big
put	dad	bow	train
mine	door	sheep	wash
C. bow	H. give	M. mine	R. dad
bed	ball	sleep	mouse
five	mouse	red	said
with	hair	food	hair
yet	big	house	book
D. sheep	I. room	N. bed	S. give
her	saw	some	cap
down	cap	yes	hen
food	stick	fat	meat
car	three	boy	stick
E. cat	J. hen	O. five	T. door
red	wash	gun	jump
dog	jump	her	three
has	one	cat	saw
gun	said	dish	floor

138

APPENDIX 3

TWO-VOWEL DISCRIMINATION TEST

ee	ir	*(Practice Items)*
ar	oo	
ee	ar	
or	ee	Key to short vowels:
oo	ee	u as in cup
ar	or	oo as in foot
		a as in cat
u	oo	i as in tin
oo	a	e as in get
i	u	
e	a	
a	u	

APPENDIX 4

COMMONWEALTH ACOUSTIC LABORATORIES ADAPTATION OF
THE MRC WORD LISTS

	List No. 1	*List No. 2*	*List No. 3*	*List No. 4*
Practice	1. your	1. glow	1. oat	1. you
Items:	2. touch	2. queer	2. fiend	2. quit
	3. frost	3. mean	3. slim	3. shift
	4. all	4. think	4. our	4. last
	5. pet	5. yawn	5. more	5. reel
Test	6. splash	6. hurl	6. bait	6. solve
Items:	7. lunge	7. thrash	7. suck	7. rear
	8. cleanse	8. dim	8. vast	8. watch
	9. nook	9. crave	9. bean	9. wrath
	10. bad	10. jam	10. job	10. punt
	11. smile	11. ball	11. trash	11. rode
	12. cane	12. lush	12. niece	12. wink
	13. there	13. why	13. pick	13. thud
	14. folk	14. path	14. bad	14. fowls
	15. hive	15. rouse	15. earl	15. choose
	16. toe	16. gnaw	16. need	16. sly
	17. rag	17. wedge	17. five	17. green
	18. grove	18. nest	18. dark	18. true
	19. are	19. please	19. log	19. pipe
	20. dish	20. rate	20. rap	20. kid
	21. is	21. neck	21. scythe	21. bathe
	22. use	22. take	22. mute	22. scare
	23. then	23. muck	23. fate	23. tug
	24. feast	24. wharf	24. frog	24. trade
	25. clove	25. trip	25. choice	25. sick
	26. like	26. sob	26. snuff	26. inch
	27. no	27. air	27. nut	27. roe (or grow)
	28. rub	28. flush	28. sludge	28. add
	29. docks	29. cast	29. blush	29. feed
	30. pants	30. ache	30. pit	30. high

	List No. 5	List No. 6	List No. 7	List No. 8
Practice Items:	1. lot	1. rum	1. now	1. quite
	2. nest	2. beg	2. jack	2. bed
	3. slop	3. mouse	3. slit	3. near
	4. yet	4. torn	4. last	4. run
	5. gag	5. win	5. town	5. wall
Test Items:	6. pulse	6. than	6. fin	6. strife
	7. fame	7. nuts	7. cloak	7. bar
	8. shout	8. toad	8. shed	8. bask
	9. pig	9. ten	9. doom	9. rise
	10. leave	10. nerve	10. rut	10. fern
	11. toil	11. fun	11. hatch	11. pan
	12. vow	12. pack	12. rack	12. fraud
	13. sped	13. thank	13. pearl	13. death
	14. oak	14. fuse	14. bush	14. rat
	15. cape	15. sip	15. float	15. slip
	16. law	16. mass	16. bath	16. creed
	17. who	17. birth	17. sage	17. deed
	18. deck	18. foe	18. test	18. end
	19. drop	19. reed	19. tick	19. crash
	20. barred	20. flag	20. pinch	20. heap
	21. class	21. noose	21. blonde	21. pest
	22. turf	22. crowd	22. starve	22. hunt
	23. bead	23. with	23. slap	23. ford
	24. check	24. chess	24. scab	24. wheat
	25. crime	25. throne	25. new	25. hid
	26. size	26. wild	26. peck	26. not
	27. far	27. arch	27. bus	27. such
	28. dig	28. ice	28. hiss	28. bride
	29. sit	29. club	29. kite	29. fuss
	30. stag	30. odd	30. course	30. pile

APPENDIX 5

ADAPTED K/T LISTS

List 1	List 2	List 3	List 4	List 5	
knife	fork	gate	duck	horse	
fish	pin	egg	boat	doll	
house	boat	sheep	cat	pig	
car	tree	mat	brick	hen	
brush	shoe	dog	ball	bus	
bus	key	match	cup	dog	
pipe	horse	wheel	pig	egg	
cow	tin	plate	mat	ball	
string	spoon	bed	fork	glove	
bath	*soap*	*watch*	*stone*	*pin*	
chair	cup	shoe	tree	man	Distractors
bird	cat	boat	cow	soap	

142

BIBLIOGRAPHY

1. AMERICAN MEDICAL ASSOCIATION (1942): Tentative standard procedure for evaluating the percentage of useful hearing loss in medicolegal cases. *JAMA, 119:*1108-1109.
2. ARONSON, A. E.; HIND, J. E., and IRWIN, J. V. (1958): GSR auditory threshold mechanisms: Effect of tonal intensity on amplitude and latency under two-tone shock intervals. *J Speech Hearing Res, 1:*211-219.
3. BANGS, J. L., and MULLINS, C. J. (1953): Recruitment testing in hearing and its implications. *Arch Otolaryng, 58:*582-592.
4. BANGS, T. E. (1954): Methodology in auditory training. *(Chicago), Volta Rev, 56:*159-164.
5. BARKER, R. G.; WRIGHT, B. A., and GONICK, M. R. (1946): *Adjustment to Physical Handicap and Illness.* New York. Social Science Research Council.
6. BECKING, A. G. T. (1953): Perception of airborne sound in the thorax of deaf children. In *Proceedings of the International Course in Paedo-Audiology.* Groningen, Groningen University.
7. BEKESY, G. (1947): The recruitment phenomenon and difference limen in hearing and vibration sense. *Laryngoscope, 57:*765-777.
8. BERANEK, L. L. (1954): *Acoustics.* New York, McGraw.
9. BOARD OF EDUCATION (1938): *Report of the Committee of Enquiry into Problems Relating to Children with Defective Hearing.* London, H.M.S.O.
10. BOOTHROYD, A. (1965): The provision of better earmoulds for deaf children. *J Laryng, 79:*320-335.
11. BRITISH STANDARDS INSTITUTION (1954): *The Normal Threshold of Hearing for Pure Tones by Earphone Listening (BS2497: 1954).* London, B.S.I.
12. BUNCH, C. C. (1940): Useable hearing. *Ann Otol, 49:*359-367.
13. BURK, K. W. (1958): Traditional and psychogalvanic skin response audiometry. *J Speech Hearing Res, 1:*275-278.
14. CARHART, R. (1946): Monitored live-voice as a test of auditory acuity. *J Acoust Soc Amer, 17:*339-349.
15. CARHART, R. (1946): Tests for the selection of hearing aids. *Laryngoscope, 56:*780-794.
16. CARHART, R. (1946c): Volume control adjustment in hearing aid selection. *Laryngoscope, 56:*510-526.

17. CARHART, R. (1947): In *Hearing and Deafness*, ed. by H. Davis. New York, Murray Hill Books.

18. CARHART, R. (1951): Basic principles of speech audiometry. *Acta Otolaryng (Stockh)*, **40:**62-71.

19. CARHART, R. (1957): Clinical determination of abnormal auditory adaptation. *Arch Otolaryng (Chicago)*, **65:**32-39.

20. CARHART, R. (1958): The usefulness of the binaural hearing aid. *J Speech Hearing Dis*, **23:**42-51.

21. CARHART, R., and JERGER, J. F. (1959): Preferred method for clinical determination of pure-tone thresholds. *J Speech Hearing Dis*, **24:** 330-345.

22. CATLIN, F. I. (1957): Stimulators for psychogalvanic testing, with special reference to clinical audiometry. *Acta Otolaryng (Stockh)*, **48:**374-378.

23. CAWTHORNE, T., and HARVEY, R. M. (1953): A comparison between hearing for pure tones and for speech. *J Laryng*, **67:**233-247.

24. CLARKE, B. R. (1952): Auditory training of profoundly deaf children. Ph.D. Thesis, Manchester University.

25. CLARKE, B. R. (1957): Use of a group hearing aid by profoundly deaf children. In *Educational Guidance and the Deaf Child*, ed. by A. W. G. Ewing. Manchester, Manchester University Press, pp. 128-159.

26. DALE, D. M. C. (1958): The possibility of providing extensive auditory experience for severely and profoundly deaf children by means of hearing aids. Ph.D. Thesis, Manchester University.

27. DALZIEL, G. H. (1954): Some procedures for obtaining maximum benefit from the use of hearing aids. *Teacher of the Deaf*, **52:**143-152.

28. DAVIS, H. (1948): The articulation area and the social adequacy index for hearing. *Laryngoscope*, **58:**761-778.

29. DAVIS, H., and KRANZ, F. (1964): International audiometric zero. *J Acoust Soc Amer*, **36:**1450-1454.

30. DAVIS, H.; HUDGINS, C. V.; MARQUIS, R. J.; NICHOLS, R. H.; PETERSON, G. E.; ROSS, D. A., and STEVENS, S. S. (1946): The selection of Hearing Aids. *Laryngoscope*, **56:**85-115 and 135-163.

31. DAVIS, H.; STEVENS, S. S.; NICHOLS, R. H.; HUDGINS, C. V.; PETERSON, G. E.; MARQUIS, R. J., and ROSS, D. A. (1947): *Hearing Aids: An Experimental Study of Design Objectives*. Cambridge, Harvard University Press.

32. DEATHERAGE, B. H. (1966): Examination of binaural interaction. *J Acoust Soc Amer*, **39:**232-249.

33. DE BRUINES-ALTES, J. C. (1946): *The Symptom of Regression in Different Kinds of Deafness*. Groningen, J. B. Wolters.

34. DENES, P., and NAUNTON, R. F. (1950): The clinical detection of auditory recruitment. *J. Laryng,* **64:**375-398.

35. DERBYSHIRE, A. J., and FARLEY, J. C. (1959): Sampling auditory responses at the cortical level. *Ann Otol,* **68:**675-697.

36. DERBYSHIRE, A. J., and McDERMOTT, M. (1958): Further contributions to the EEG method of evaluating auditory function. *Laryngoscope,* **68:**558-570.

37. DIX, M. R.; HALLPIKE, C. S., and HOOD, J. D. (1948): Observations upon the loudness recruitment phenomenon with especial reference to the differential diagnosis of disorders of the internal ear and VIIIth nerve. *J Laryng,* **62:**671-686.

38. DIX, M. R.; HALLPIKE, C. S., and HOOD, J. D. (1949): Nerve deafness: its clinical criteria, old and new. *J Laryng,* **63:**685-698.

39. DIX, M. R., and HOOD, J. D. (1953): Modern developments in pure tone audiometry and their application to the clinical diagnosis of end-organ deafness. *J Laryng,* **67:**343-357.

40. EBY, L. G., and WILLIAMS, H. L. (1951): Recruitment of loudness in the differential diagnosis of end-organ and nerve fibre deafness. *Laryngoscope,* **61:**400-414.

41. EDGARDH, B. H. (1951-52): The use of extreme limitation for the dynamic equalization of vowels and consonants in hearing aids. *Acta Otolaryng (Stockh),* **40:**376-382.

42. EGAN, J. P. (1944): Articulation testing methods. II OSRD. Report No. 3802. Psycho-Acoustic Laboratory, Harvard University, Cambridge (Mass.). Quoted by Beranek (1954).[8]

43. EGAN, J. P. (1948): Articulation testing methods. *Laryngoscope,* **58:**955-991.

44. EWERTSEN, H. W.; IPSEN, J. B., and NIELSEN, S. S. (1957): On acoustical characteristics of the ear-mould. *Acta Otolaryng (Stockh),* **47:**312-317.

45. EWERTSEN, H. W., and NIELSEN, M. (1957): Soft earmould. *Acta Otolaryng (Stockh),* **47:**231-232.

46. EWING, A. W. G. (1940): In the discussion on Audiometric tests and the capacity to hear speech. *Proc Roy Soc Med,* **33:**237-244.

47. EWING, A. W. G. (1947): Hearing aids and clinics in England. *Laryngoscope,* **57:**41-44.

48. EWING, A. W. G. (1947): Hearing aids for the deaf. *Practitioner,* **158:**129-138.

49. EWING, A. W. G. (1956): History of the department of education of the deaf, University of Manchester, 1919-1955. *Brit J Educ Studies,* **4:**103-128.

50. EWING, A. W. G. (Ed.) (1957): *Educational Guidance and the Deaf Child.* Manchester, Manchester University Press.

51. EWING, A. W. G. (Ed.) (1960): *The Modern Educational Treatment of Deafness.* Manchester, Manchester University Press.
52. EWING, A. W. G., and EWING, E. C. (1964): *Teaching deaf children to talk.* Manchester, Manchester University Press.
53. EWING, A. W. G.; EWING, I. R., and LITTLER, T. S. (1936): The use of hearing aids. Medical Research Council, Special Report Series, No. 219, London, H.M.S.O.
54. EWING, A. W. G., and LITTLER, T. S. (1935): Auditory fatigue and adaptation. *Brit J Psychol,* **25:**284-307.
55. EWING, I. R. (1946): *Lipreading and Hearing Aids.* Manchester, Manchester University Press.
56. EWING, I. R., and EWING, A. W. G. (1938): *The Handicap of Deafness.* London, Longman, Green & Co.
57. EWING, I. R., and EWING, A. W. G. (1944): The ascertainment of deafness in infancy and early childhood. *J Laryng,* **59:**309-333.
58. EWING, I. R., and EWING, A. W. G. (1954): *Speech and the Deaf Child.* Manchester, Manchester University Press.
59. EWING, I. R., and EWING, A. W. G. (1958): *New Opportunities for Deaf Children.* London, University of London Press.
60. FANT, G. (1948): Analys av de svenska vokalljuden. *L.M.E. Report,* No. 1035, Stockholm.
61. FANT, G. (1948): Analys av de svenska konsonantjuden. *L.M.E. Report,* No. 1064, Stockholm.
62. FLETCHER, H. (1929): *Speech and Hearing in Communication.* New York, Van Nostrand. (Reprinted 1953).
63. FLETCHER, H. (1950): A method of calculating hearing loss for speech from an audiogram. *Acta Otolaryng (Stockh), Suppl.* **90:** 26-37.
64. FLETCHER, H., and STEINBERG, J. C. (1930): Articulation testing methods. *J Acoust Soc Amer, 1*(2, pt. 2), 1-97.
65. FOWLER, E. P. (1937): The diagnosis of diseases of the neural mechanism of hearing by the aid of sounds well above threshold. *Laryngoscope,* **47:**289-300.
66. FOWLER, E. P. (1946): Report to the sub-committee on the evaluation of individual hearing aids in public schools. *Amer Ann Deaf,* **91:**397-402.
67. FOWLER, E. P. (1947): In *Hearing and Deafness,* ed. by H. Davis. New York, Murray Hill Books.
68. FOWLER, E. P. (1950): Recruitment of loudness phenomenon. *Laryngoscope,* **60:**680-695.
69. FOWLER, E. P.; LORGE, I., and STANTON, M. B. (1946): The value of individual hearing aids for hard of hearing children in public schools. *Laryngoscope,* **56:**26-32.

70. FRENCH, N. R., and STEINBERG, J. C. (1947): Factors governing the intelligibility of speech sounds. *J Acoust Soc Amer, 19:*90-119.
71. FRY, D. B., and KERRIDGE, P. M. J. (1939): Tests for the hearing of speech by deaf people. *Lancet, 1:*106-109.
72. FRY, D. B., and WHETNALL, E. (1954): The auditory approach in training of deaf children. *Lancet, 1:*583-587.
73. GASKILL, P. (1952): *The Educational Guidance of School Children with Defective Hearing.* M.Ed. Thesis, Manchester University.
74. GETZ, S. B. (1955): The factor of hereditary deafness in auditory training. *Acta Otolaryng (Stockh), 45:*395-397.
75. GLASSEY, W., and WEEKS, E. J. (1950): *The Educational Development of Children.* London, University of London Press.
76. GOODMAN, A. I. (1949): Residual capacity to hear of pupils in schools for the deaf. *J Laryng, 63:*551-579.
77. GOLDSTEIN, M. A. (1939): *The Acoustic Method for the Training of the Deaf and Hard of Hearing Child.* St. Louis, The Laryngoscope Press.
78. GRAHAM, A. B. (1960): Hearing aids: major determinates of their effectiveness. *Hearing News, 28*(5):9-12.
79. GUILFORD, F. R. (1954): Hearing rehabilitation in private practice. *Arch Otolaryng, 60:*490-500.
80. GUILFORD, J. P. (1956): *Fundamental Statistics in Psychology and Education,* 3rd. ed. New York, McGraw.
81. GROEN, J. J., and TAPPIN, J. W. (1952): A comparison of the physical characteristics of five well known hearing aids with the theoretical and apparent subjective needs of the patient. *J Laryng, 66:*604-613.
82. HANLEY, C. N.; TIFFANY, W. R., and BRUNGARD, J. M. (1958): Skin resistance changes accompanying the side tone test for auditory malingering. *J Speech Hearing Res, 1:*286-293.
83. HARBERT, F., and SATALOFF, J. A. (1955): Clinical application of recruitment and masking. *Laryngoscope, 65:*113-123.
84. HARDY, W. G., and BORDLEY, J. E. (1951): Special techniques in testing the hearing of children. PGSR audiometry. *J Speech Hearing Dis, 16:*125-131.
85. HARDY, W. G., and PAULS, M. D. (1959): Significance of problems of conditioning in GSR audiometry. *J Speech Hearing Dis, 24:*123-126.
86. HAROLD, B. B. (1957): The effect of variations in intensity on the capacity of deaf children and adults to hear speech with hearing aids. Ph.D. Thesis, Manchester University.
87. HASKINS, H. L., and HARDY, W. G. (1960): Clinical studies in stereophonic hearing. *Laryngoscope, 70:*1427-1432.

88. Hirsh, I. J. (1951): Audiology and the basic sciences. *Acta Otolaryng (Stockh),* **40**:42-50.

89. Hirsh, I. J. (1952): *The Measurement of Hearing.* New York, McGraw.

90. Hirsh, I. J., and Ward, W. D. (1952): Recovery of the auditory threshold after strong acoustic stimulation. *J Acoust Soc Amer,* **24**:131-141.

91. Hirsh, I. J.; Palva, T., and Goodman, A. (1954): Difference limen and recruitment. *Arch Otolaryng,* **60**:525-540.

92. Hood, J. D. (1950): Studies in auditory fatigue and adaptation. *Acta Otolaryng (Stockh), Suppl. 92.*

93. Hudgins, C. V. (1948): A rationale for acoustic training. *Volta Rev,* **50**:484-490.

94. Hudgins, C. V. (1953): The response of profoundly deaf children to auditory training. *J Speech Hearing Dis,* **18**:273-288.

95. Hudgins, C. V. (1954): Auditory training: Its possibilities and limitations. *Volta Rev,* **56**:339-349.

96. Hudgins, C. V. (1958): Personal communication.

97. Hudgins, C. V.; Hawkins, J. E.; Karlin, J. E., and Stevens, S. S. (1947): The development of recorded auditory tests for measuring hearing loss for speech. *Laryngoscope,* **57**:57-89.

98. Hudgins, C. V.; Marquis, R. J.; Nichols, R. H.; Peterson, G. E., and Ross, D. A. (1948): The comparative performance of an experimental hearing aid and two commercial instruments. *J Acoust Soc Amer,* **20**:241-258.

99. Hughson, W., and Westlake, H. (1944): Manual for programme outline for rehabilitation of aural casualties both military and civil. *Trans Amer Acad Ophthal Otolaryng, Suppl.* **48**:1-15.

100. Hughson, W.; Ciocco, A.; Witting, E. G., and Lawrence, P. S. (1941): An analysis of speech characteristics in deafened children, with observations on training methods. *Laryngoscope,* **51**:868-891.

101. Huizing, H. (1951): Auditory training. *Acta Otolaryng (Stockh), Suppl.* **100**:158-163.

102. Huizing, H. (1951-52): The recruitment factor in hearing tests. *Acta Otolaryng (Stockh),* **40**:297-306.

103. Ingall, B. I. (1963): An address, *Teacher of the Deaf,* **61**:24-36.

104. Irwin, J. V.; Hind, J. E., and Aronson, A. E. (1957): *Training School Bull,* **54**:26-31. Item No. 5001 in *Psychol Abstr,* **32**:1958, 452.

105. Jerger, J. F. (1952): A difference limen recruitment test and its diagnostic significance. *Laryngoscope,* **62**:1316-1332.

106. Jerger, J. F. (1953): DL difference test—improved method for clinical measurement of recruitment. *Arch Otolaryng,* **57**:490-500.

107. JERGER, J. F. (1953): A new test for cochlear reserve in the selection of patients for fenestration surgery. *Ann Otol, 62:*724-734.

108. JERGER, J. F. (1955): Differential intensity sensitivity in ear with loudness recruitment. *J Speech Hearing Dis, 20:*183-191.

109. JERGER, J. F., and DIRKS, D. (1961): Binaural hearing aids—an enigma. *J Acoust Soc Amer, 33:*537-538.

110. JOHANSSON, B. (1959): A new coding amplifier system for the severely hard of hearing. *Proc 3rd Inter Congr Acoustics,* Stuttgart, Elsevier, Amsterdam, 1961. *Vol. 2:* pp. 655-7.

111. JOHANSSON, B. (1966): *The use of the transposer for the management of the deaf child.* Stockholm, Karolinska Institutet.

112. JOHN, J. E. J.: Hearing aids and classroom acoustics. *Teacher of the Deaf, 51:*103-110; 141-146.

113. JOHN, J. E. J. (1957): Acoustics and efficiency in the use of hearing aids. In *Educational Guidance and the Deaf Child,* ed. by A. W. G. Ewing. Manchester, Manchester University Press, pp. 160-175.

114. JOHN, J. E. J., and HOWARTH, J. N. (1965): The effect of time distortions on the intelligibility of deaf children's speech. *Language and Speech, 8:*127-134.

115. JOHN, J. E. J., and THOMAS, H. (1957): Design and construction of schools for the deaf. In *Educational Guidance and the Deaf Child,* ed. by A. W. G. Ewing. Manchester, Manchester University Press, pp. 176-187.

116. JUERS, A. L. (1956): Pure tone threshold and hearing for speech diagnostic significance of inconsistencies. *Laryngoscope, 66:*402-409.

117. JUSTMAN, J., and MOSKOWITZ, S. (1956): *The Integration of Deaf Children in a Hearing Class.* Board of Education of the City of New York, Publication no. 36.

118. Kay Electric Co. (1950): *Instruction Manual—The Sona-graph.* Pine Brook, N.J., Kay Electric Co.

119. KENDALL, D. C. (1953): The mental development of young deaf children. Ph.D. Thesis, Manchester University.

120. KENDALL, D. C. (1956): In the discussion on the management of deafness in the young child. *Proc Roy Soc Med, 49:*463-467.

121. KNIGHT, J. J., and LITTLER, T. S. (1953): The technique of speech audiometry and a simple speech audiometer with masking generator for clinical use. *J Laryng, 67:*248-265.

122. KNUDSEN, V. O., and HARRIS, C. M. (1950): *Acoustical Designing in Architecture.* New York, Wiley.

123. KNUDSEN, V. O.; SEPMEYER, L. W., and WATSON, L. A. (1936): Selective amplification aids to hearing. *J Acoust Soc Amer, 7:*235.

124. KOBRAK, H. G. (1957): Objective audiometry: utilization of an un-
conditioned muscle reflex for the determination of sound perception. *Arch Otolaryng,* **65:**26-31.

125. LEHRHOFF, I. (1958): An experimental study of auditory threshold
acuity in children with cerebral palsy, by PGSR and other techniques. *Ann Otol,* **67:**643-654.

126. LICKLIDER, J. C. R. (1946): Effects of amplitude distortion upon the
intelligibility of speech. *J Acoust Soc Amer,* **18:**429-434.

127. LIDEN, G. (1954): Speech audiometry—an experimental and clinical
study with Swedish language material. *Acta Otolaryng (Stockh),*
Suppl. 114.

128. LING, D. (1964): Implications of hearing aid amplification below
300c.p.s. *Volta Rev,* **66:**723-729.

129. LITTLER, T. S. (1936): Hearing aids for the deaf. *J Sci Instrum,* **13:**
144-155.

130. LITTLER, T. S. (1944): Electrical hearing aids. *J Instn Elect Engrs,*
91:67-74.

131. LITTLER, T. S. (1954): Hearing tests and hearing aids. In *Modern*
Trends in Diseases of the Ear, Nose and Throat, ed. by M. Ellis.
London, Butterworths, pp. 58-69.

132. LONGWORTH, A. (1957): The first year in the nursery school. *Teacher*
of the Deaf, **55:**50-55.

133. LOWELL, E., and STONER, M. (1960): *Play it by Ear.* Los Angeles,
John Tracy Clinic.

134. LUNDBORG, T. (1952): The Bekesy audiogram in the differential diagnosis between end organ and nerve fibre deafness. *Acta*
Otolaryng (Stockh), Suppl. **99:**1-111.

135. LURIE, M. H. (1940): Studies of acquired and inherited deafness in
animals. *J Acoust Soc Amer,* **11:**420-426.

136. LUSCHER, E., and ZWISLOCKI, J. (1948): A simple method for indi-
rect monaural determination of the recruitment phenomenon. *Acta*
Otolaryng (Stockh), Suppl. **78:**156-168.

137. Medical Research Council (1947): Hearing aids and audiometers.
Special Report Series no. 261. London, H.M.S.O.

138. MEUNARGIYA, R. V. (1958): Hearing acuity with the aid of electro-
cardiography. *Vestn Otorinlaring,* **20:**14-19. Abstract no. 862.
Excerpta Med (Amst), **12:**1959, 161.

139. MIDGLEY, J. D. (1957): Screening tests of hearing in primary schools.
In *In Educational Guidance and the Deaf Child,* ed. by A. W. G.
Ewing. Manchester, Manchester University Press, pp. 107-127.

140. MILLER, G. A. (1951): *Language and Communication.* New York,
McGraw.

141. Ministry of Education (1946): Special educational treatment. Pam-
phlet No. 5. London, H.M.S.O.

142. Ministry of Education (1956): The health of the school child. Report of the Chief Medical Officer to the Ministry of Education. London, H.M.S.O.

143. MOSER, H. M., and DREHER, J. J. (1955): Effects of training on listeners in intelligibility studies. *J Acoust Soc Amer*, **27**:1213-1219.

144. MULLINS, C. J., and BANGS, J. L. (1957): Relationships between speech discrimination and other audiometric data. *Acta Otolaryng (Stockh)*, **47**:149-157.

145. MURPHY, K. P. (1956): A survey of the intelligence and abilities of twelve-year-old deaf children. Ph.D. Thesis, Manchester University.

146. MURPHY, L. J. (1950): Assessment of the abilities of deaf children. Ph.D. Thesis, Manchester University.

147. MURRAY, N. E. (1959): *Auditory Equipment for Educational Purposes.* Commonwealth Acoustic Laboratories, Sydney, Australia. (Unpublished statement.)

148. MURRAY, N. E. (1952): *Speech Tests of Hearing.* Report I.R.4. Commonwealth Acoustic Laboratories, Sydney, Australia.

149. MURRAY, N. E. (1953): Ultimate limitations of hearing aids. *Proc Fifth Conference of Teachers of the Deaf in Australia.*

150. MYGIND, S. H. (1952): The function and the diseases of the labyrinth. *Acta Otolaryng (Stockh)*, **41**:235-325.

151. MYKLEBUST, H. R. (1946): The use of individual hearing aids in schools for the deaf. *Amer Ann Deaf*, **91**:255-261.

152. NEWBY, A. H. (1958): *Audiology—Its Data and First Principles.* New York, Appleton.

153. NILSSON, G. (1942): Some aspects of the differential diagnosis of obstructive and neural deafness. *Acta Otolaryng (Stockh)*, **30**:125-138.

154. NUMBERS, M. E., and HUDGINS, C. V.: Speech perception in present day education for deaf children. *Volta Rev*, **50**:449-456.

155. O'CONNOR, C. D. (1940): The use of residual hearing. *Volta Rev*, **42**:327-333.

156. PALMER, J. M. (1955): The effect of speaker differences on the intelligibility of phonetically balanced word lists. *J Speech Hearing Dis*, **20**:192-195.

157. PALVA, T. (1952): Finnish speech audiometry. *Acta Otolaryng (Stockh)*, **Suppl. 101.**

158. PALVA, T. (1955): Studies on per-stimulatory adaptation in various groups of deafness. *Laryngoscope*, **65**:829-847.

159. Philips Electrical Limited (1960): *Statement Regarding High Frequency Response of Insert Type Receivers.* Holland, Eindhoven.

160. PICKLES, A. M. (1957): Home training with hearing aids. In *Educational Guidance and the Deaf Child*, ed. by A. W. G. Ewing, Manchester, Manchester University Press, pp. 77-104.

161. PIMONOW, L. (1966): Parole synthetique et son application practique. *C R Acad Sci (Paris)*, **262**, *(Series D)*:672-674.

162. PLANT, G. R. G. (1960): The Plant-Mandy voice trainer. *Teacher of the Deaf*, **58**:12-15.

163. QUICK, M. A. (1953): A test for measuring achievement in speech perception among young deaf children. *Volta Rev*, **55**:28-31.

164. REED, M. (1960): R.N.I.D. Hearing Test Cards. R.N.I.D., 105 Gower St., London, W.C.1.

165. REGER, S. N. (1935): Loudness level contours and intensity discrimination of ears with raised auditory thresholds. *J Acoust Soc Amer*, **7**:73.

166. RICE, G. C. (1964): Hearing aid design criteria. In *Proc Seventh Inter Congr Audiology*, Copenhagen.

167. RISBERG, A. (1965): The transposer and a model of speech perception. *Quarterly Progress and Status Reports*, Speech Transmission Laboratory, Stockholm (STL-QPSR-4/1965 pp. 26-30).

168. RONNEI, E. C. (1951): *Learning to Look and Listen*. New York, Teachers College, Columbia University.

169. RUHM, H. B., and CARHART, R. B. (1958): Objective speech audiometry: A new method based on electrodermal response. *J Speech Hearing Res*, **1**:169-178.

170. SCHONELL, F. J., and SCHONELL, F. E. (1950): *Diagnostic and Attainment Testing*. Edinburgh, Oliver and Boyd.

171. SCHUKNECHT, H. F., and WOELLNER, R. G. (1955): An experimental and clinical study of deafness from lesions of the cochlea nerve. *J Laryng*, **69**:75-97.

172. SIEGENTHALER, B. M., and GUNN, G. H. (1952): Factors associated with help obtained from individual hearing aids. *J Speech Hearing Dis*, **17**:338-347.

173. SILVERMAN, S. R. (1944): Training for optimum use of hearing aids. *Laryngoscope*, **54**:29-36.

174. SILVERMAN, S. R. (1947): Tolerance for pure tones and speech in normal and defective ears. *Ann Otol*, **56**:658-677.

175. SILVERMAN, S. R. (1949): The implications for schools for the deaf of recent research on hearing aids. *Amer Ann Deaf*, **94**:325-339.

176. SILVERMAN, S. R., and HARRISON, C. E. (1951): The national research council group hearing aid project. *Amer Ann Deaf*, **96**:420-431.

177. SOKOLOV, E. N., and PARAMONOVA, N. P. (1959): Objective examination of the residual hearing of deaf children. *Beltone Translation*, No. 10, Feb. 1959, from *Ostatochnyi Slukh u Tugoukhikh i Glukhoneymykh Detei*, Academy of Pedagogic Sciences RSFSR, Moscow.

178. SORTINI, A. J. (1957): Skin-response audiometry for pre-school children. *J Speech Hearing Dis,* **22:**241-244.
179. STEINBERG, J. C., and GARDNER, M. (1937): The dependence of hearing impairment on sound intensity. *J Acoust Soc Amer,* **9:**11-23.
180. TUMARKIN, A. (1935): Scientific audiometry and selective amplification in the design and construction of modern deaf-aids. *J Laryng,* **50:**838-847.
181. TUMARKIN, A. (1950): The decibel, the phon and the sone. *J Laryng,* **64:**178-188.
182. TUMARKIN, A. (1954): The decibel, the phon and the sone. Part 2. *J Laryng,* **68:**411-428.
183. UDEN, A. VAN (1955): Rhythmic training in sound perception with severely deaf children. Address to N.C.T.D. Conference, Besley and Copp, Exeter.
184. UDEN, A. VAN (1957): Personal communication.
185. UDEN, A. VAN (1960): Sound perceptive method. In *The Modern Educational Treatment of Deafness,* ed. by A. W. G. Ewing. Manchester, Manchester University Press, pp. 3-12.
186. WALKER, A. S. (1955): *Pupils schools records.* London National Foundation for Educational Research.
187. WALSH, T. E., and SILVERMAN, S. R. (1946): Diagnosis and evaluation of fenestration. *Laryngoscope,* **56:**536-555.
188. WARD, I. C. (1952): *The Phonetics of English.* Cambridge, Heffer.
189. WATSON, L. A. (1944): Certain fundamental principles in prescribing and fitting hearing aids. *Laryngoscope,* **54:**531-538.
190. WATSON, L. A., and TOLAN, T. (1949): *Hearing Tests and Hearing Instruments.* Baltimore, Williams & Wilkins.
191. WATSON, N. A. (1940): Selective amplification in hearing aids. *J Acoust Soc Amer,* **11:**377-378.
192. WATSON, T. J. (1955): *The Use of Group Hearing Aids in Auditory Training.* Besley and Copp, Exeter.
193. WATSON, T. J. (1957): Speech audiometry for children. In *Educational Guidance and the Deaf Child,* ed. by A. W. G. Ewing. Manchester, Manchester University Press, pp. 278-296.
194. WATSON, T. J. (1958): Some factors affecting the successful use of hearing aids by deaf children. In *The Modern Educational Treatment of Deafness,* ed. by A. W. G. Ewing. Manchester, Manchester University Press, Chapter 34, pp. 34/1-5.
195. WATTS, A. F. (1946): *The Language and Mental Development of Children.* London, Harrap.
196. WECHSLER, D. (1944): *Measurement of Adult Intelligence.* Baltimore, Williams & Wilkins.
197. WEDENBERG, E. (1951): Auditory training of deaf and hard of hearing children. *Acta Otolaryng (Stockh), Suppl.* **94:**1-130.

198. WEDENBERG, E. (1954): Auditory training of severely hard of hearing pre-school children. *Acta Otolaryng (Stockh), Suppl. 110:*7-81.

199. WEGEL, R. L., and LANE, C. E. (1924): The auditory masking of one pure tone by another and its probable relation to the dynamics of the inner ear. *Physical Rev, 2nd series, 23:*266-285.

200. WEVER, E. G. (1957): *Theory of Hearing.* New York, Wiley.

201. WHETNALL, E. (1949): The medresco in the service of a deafness clinic. *J Laryng, 63:*742-755.

202. WHIPPLE, C. I., and KODMAN, F. (1960): The validity of objective speech audiometry. *J Laryng, 74:*84-89.

203. WHITEHURST, M. W. (1947): Training the hearing of a young deaf child—(Louise, aged 5½). *Volta Rev, 49:*215, 252.

204. WHITEHURST, M. W. (1949): *Auditory Training for Children.* New York Hearing Rehabilitation Center.

205. WITHROW, F. B., and GOLDSTEIN, R. (1958): An electrophysiologic procedure for determination of auditory threshold in children. *Laryngoscope, 68:*1674-1699.

206. YENRICK, D. E. (1955): Audiology and the deaf child. *Volta Rev, 57:*353-356.

INDEX

A

Accent, 69
Acoustic conditions, 75-83
Acoustic feedback, 126-128
Adapted M/J words, 37, 38, 138
Adults, use of hearing aids, 114
Aetiology, 48, 104
Air conduction testing, 27-30
American Medical Association
   percentage scale, 53
Amplification, 4-14
  electrical, 4
  level of, 41, 83-95
  selective, 9
Amplifier, 4, 130
Announcers, radio, 71, 72, 75
  radio and television, 5, 6
Articulation
  curves, 83-85, 89
  score, 83
Artificial ear, 94
Audibility, threshold of, 13
Audiogram, 26, 60
  fitting, 8
  hearing for speech, 47-57
  interpretation, 48-52, 60, 90-93
  shadow, 31
  shape of, 48, 51, 52
Audiometers, 25-27
  calibration, 13
  speech circuit, 43, 90
  von Bekesy, 101, 102
Auditory experience, 106-135
  training, 108
Automatic volume control, 11

B

Bangs, T. E., 86
Bangs, J. and Mullins, C., 101
Batteries, 125
  tension, 8
Beat, 101

Becking, A., 108
Beranek, L. L., 72
Binaural listening, 14-16
Bone conduction testing, 30, 31, 32,
   45, 104
British Medical Research Council, 9

C

Carhart, R., 47, 84, 87, 90, 106
Carhart, R. and Jerger, J. F., 27
Cawthorn, T. and Harvey, R. M., 47,
   48
Checking of aids, 114-116
Clarke, B., 110
Clinical audiometry, 42-46
Clothes rub, 122
Commonwealth Acoustic Laboratories
   (Australia), 34, 38
Compression amplification, 11-12
Conductive deafness, and hearing for
   speech, 85
  and recruitment, 104
Consonants, 63-68
Cycle, 4

D

Dale, D. M. C., 35, 72-75, 89-93, 112
Davis, H., 85
Davis, H., et al., 9
Deafness
  conductive, 46, 72, 85
  perceptive, 46, 72, 85
  profound, 52-53, 55, 86, 87, 108,
   109
  total, 53, 54, 55
  unilateral, 104
De Bruine Altes, J., 96, 99
Denes, P., Naunton, R., 101
Department of Audiology and Educa-
   tion of the Deaf, Manchester
   University, 9, 20, 40, 86
Detectability, threshold of, 13, 86